The Control of Private Rented Dwellings

The Control of Private Rented Dwellings

SECOND EDITION

MARK DE BLÁCAM

MA, Barrister-at-law

THE ROUND HALL PRESS

This book was typeset by
Gilbert Gough Typesetting, Dublin
for The Round Hall Press Ltd,
Kill Lane, Blackrock, Co. Dublin.

A catalogue record for this book
is available from the British Library.

ISBN 0-947686-87-8
0-947686-88-6 pbk

Printed in England
by Billing & Son Ltd, Worcester

Contents

Preface

'The object of this book is,' as I said in the preface to the first edition, 'to explain the present-day Irish law on the control of rented dwellings.' That general object remains unchanged. But in writing this second edition I have specifically set out to up-date the book to take account of developments in the law since the publication of the first edition in 1984. I have also decided to add a new chapter on the history of rent control. The Rent Acts should be seen as a continuum. Although the starting point for the modern law is the Rent Restrictions Act 1960, many features of the present law are grounded in the earlier Acts going back to the Increase of Rent and Mortgage Interest (War Restrictions) Act 1915.

Finally, I have in this edition looked in some detail at the work and operation of the Rent Tribunal. In this regard I would like to express my thanks to Paul Kenny, the secretary of the Tribunal, for his help. My thanks are also due to two colleagues, Padraig Dwyer and Raghnal O'Riordan, both of whom not only proof-read the text but also made useful suggestions. Once again I thank Michael Adams for his help in preparing the book for publication.

MARK DE BLÁCAM

1 March 1992

ONE

The history of rent control

The beginning Rent control was introduced by the Increase of Rent and Mortgage Interest (War Restrictions) Act 1915. 'The first Rent Act of 1915 was passed . . . to protect humble homes. It did not extend to business premises. The object was to prevent landlords from taking advantage of the house famine that was only too justly expected to result from the world war to exact rents that would present humble tenants with the sole alternative of being rendered homeless or meeting the landlords' demands (if, indeed, they could meet them at all) by stinting themselves and their families of the bare necessities of life.'[1] In Ireland the 1915 Act applied to a house or a part of a house let as a separate dwelling other than one let at a rent which included payments in respect of board, attendance, or use of furniture; provided the letting did not include any land other than the site of the dwellinghouse and a garden, and provided the annual amount of the 'standard rent' or the rateable value did not exceed £26. The 'standard rent' was the rent payable on 3 August 1914, or, in the case of a dwelling first let after that date, the rent at which it was first let.

The 1915 Act rendered irrecoverable any increase on the standard rent or, in the case of a mortgage,[2] the standard rate of interest (again, generally, the rate applicable on 3 August 1914). There were, however, limited exceptions; for example, an increase was allowed where the landlord had incurred expenditure on the improvement or structural alteration of the dwelling. The Act also prohibited the making of an order for the recovery of possession of a dwellinghouse to which it applied so long as the tenant continued to pay the proper rent and performed the other conditions of the tenancy. Possession could, however, be recovered where 'the tenant has committed waste or has been guilty of conduct which is a nuisance or an annoyance to adjoining or neighbouring occupiers, or (on the ground) that the premises are reasonably required by the landlord for the occupation of himself or some other person

1. Per Black J in *Mason v Leavy* [1952] IR 40, 51.
2. The application of this and subsequent Acts to mortgages was a corollary to their application to tenancies in that a landlord, whose right to recover an increase in rent was restricted, would himself be protected against an increase in mortgage interest payable by him.

in his employ, or in the employ of some tenant from him, or on some other ground which may be deemed satisfactory by the court . . .' In the case of a mortgage to which the Act applied, a prohibition was placed on the mortgagee calling in the mortgage or taking any steps for exercising a right of foreclosure or sale. It is noteworthy that the 1915 Act expressly provided that it should 'continue in force during the continuance of the present war and for a period of six months thereafter and no longer . . .'

In 1918 the Act was amended by the Increase of Rent, &c. (Amendment) Act of that year. The 1918 Act was designed to curb the activities of persons known in England as 'bomb-dodgers' who bought dwellings occupied by tenants and sought possession 'for the occupation of (themselves)'. It did so by restricting the right to recover possession in the case of a person who became a landlord by acquiring a dwellinghouse to which the 1915 Act applied after 30 September 1917, unless he did so under a settlement made before that date, or under a testamentary disposition or an intestacy. In 1919 there were two further amendments to the 1915 Act. The first, the Increase of Rent and Mortgage Interest (Restrictions) Act 1919, extended until 25 March 1921 the application of the 1915 Act but allowed the landlord a ten per cent. increase of the standard rent. It furthermore brought within the scope of the 1915 Act a house in Ireland whose annual standard rent and rateable value exceeded £26, but neither of which exceeded £52. But it excluded from control houses erected after or in the course of erection at the passing of the Act, 2 April 1919. The second Act of 1919, the Increase of Rent, &c. (Amendment) Act of that year, was principally concerned with adjusting the grounds on which a landlord could recover possession.

There followed the Increase of Rent and Mortgage Interest (Restrictions) Act 1920 which repealed the earlier Acts and which was described in the preamble as '[a]n Act to consolidate and amend the Law with the respect to increase of rent and recovery of possession of premises in certain cases . . .' In Ireland the 1920 Act applied where either the annual amount of the standard rent or the rateable value did not exceed £78. But it did not apply to a dwellinghouse bona fide let at a rent which included payments in respect of board, attendance, or use of furniture; nor, generally, did it apply to a house let together with land other than the site of the house. Also outside the Act was a dwellinghouse erected or in the course of erection on 2 April 1919, and a dwellinghouse which had since that date been, or was at that date being, bona fide reconstructed by way of conversion into two or more separate and self-contained flats. The 1920 Act for the first time brought under control 'any premises used for business trade or professional purposes . . .' Further it provided that its application was not to be excluded by reason only that part of the premises was used as a shop or office or for business purposes.

Once again any increase, other than a permitted one, on the 'standard rent' or 'standard rate of interest', in the case of a mortgage, was rendered irrecoverable; and again the 'standard rent' and 'standard rate of interest' were, generally, fixed by reference to the amount payable on 3 August 1914. Permitted increases in rent were allowed where the landlord incurred expenditure on the improvement or structural alteration of the dwellinghouse and where the amount payable by the landlord in respect of rates was increased. The 1920 also introduced the notion of the 'net rent'. This was the standard rent less the amount of any rates paid by the landlord at the time the standard rent was calculated. In relation to this 'net rent' the landlord was, under the Act allowed a general increase not exceeding 15 per cent. Where he was responsible for the whole of the repairs, he was allowed an increase not exceeding 25 per cent. of the 'net rent'; if he was responsible for part of the repairs, he was allowed a lesser increase. The restrictions on the landlord's right to recover possession found in the earlier Acts were in large measure re-enacted, as were the restrictions on the calling in of mortgages.

The first Irish legislation The 1920 Act expired on 24 June 1923 and was replaced by the Increase of Rent and Mortgage Interest (Restrictions) Act 1923[3] enacted by the Oireachtas of Saorstát Éireann. This Act applied to a house or part of a house where either the annual amount of the standard rent or the rateable value did not exceed £60 in Dublin and £40 elsewhere; by reducing these figures from that of £78 fixed by the 1920 Act the 1923 Act effected a measure of decontrol. Again outside the Act was a furnished house, or one let together with land other than the site of the house; as was a house erected after, or in the course of erection on, 2 April 1919; a dwelling since that date, or at that date being, reconstructed by way of conversion into two or more separate and self-contained flats; and a dwellinghouse provided by a local authority under various statutory provisions. The 1923 Act continued the application of control to business premises, provided they were not held under a tenancy from year to year or for a term of years, and subject to certain modifications in relation to permitted increases and the recovery of possession. Nor, it was provided, did partial user for business, trade or professional purposes exclude control.

Under the 1923 Act the rent payable by the tenant was, generally, that which had been paid immediately prior to the commencement of the Act. The 1923 Act however, abandoned the 1920 Act term 'net rent' and redefined the 'standard rent' as that 'which in the year ending 3 August 1914, the immediate landlord of an occupying tenant of the dwellinghouse might reasonably have expected under any given contract of tenancy not being for more than a term of five years'. If the dwelling was on that date let to an

3. See Hughes, *The Increase of Rent and Mortgage Interest (Restrictions) Act 1923* (Dublin, 1923).

occupying tenant under such a contract of tenancy, then the rent at which it was so let was to be the 'standard rent', subject to a deduction for rates paid by the landlord; otherwise a court could, on the application of either party, determine the standard rent. Permitted increases of rent were, as before, allowed where the landlord incurred expenditure on the improvement or structural alteration of the dwelling; where rates were payable by the landlord; and where the landlord expended money on repairs. In addition, the Act allowed a general increase of an amount not exceeding ten per cent. of the standard rent.

The 1923 Act continued to restrict mortgage interest, subject to a permitted increase, and the calling in of mortgages; and substantially re-enacted the 1920 Act restrictions on the landlord's right to recover possession. But excluded from these restrictions was a dwellinghouse let to a tenant during his continuance in any office, appointment or employment, or for the temporary convenience or to meet a temporary necessity, either of the landlord or tenant.

Amendments and emergency powers The 1923 Act was first amended by the Increase of Rent and Mortgage Interest (Restrictions) Act 1926 which set out to effect gradual decontrol. The 1926 Act provided for a progressive reduction in the standard rent and rateable value limits for control, first to £40 in Dublin and £30 elsewhere, to £30 and £25 for the year ending 24 June 1928, and to £25 and £20 for the year ending 24 June 1929. The 1926 Act also decontrolled houses whose rateable value and standard rent exceeded £20 where the landlord came into possession on or after 24 June 1926.[4] But gradual decontrol was arrested by the Increase of Rent and Mortgage Interest (Restrictions) Act 1928 and subsequent Acts which combined to fix the limits for control at £30 in Dublin and £25 elsewhere.

Wartime conditions led once more to an increased level of control, this time implemented by the Emergency Powers (No. 313) Order 1944 which raised the limits for control to £60 in Dublin and, for the first time, Dun Laoghaire, and to £40 elsewhere. The 1944 Order reimposed control on dwellings which had been decontrolled by Acts after the 1923 Act and imposed control for the first time on houses which had been built since 1919. A further Order,[5] implemented the following year, excluded from control premises erected after, or in the course of erection on, 8 February 1944, or bona fide reconstructed into self-contained flats on or after that date. Premises brought within control by the 1944 Order had their rents restricted to the rent payable on 7 May 1941 less the amount of any rates paid by the

4. See *Donnelly v O'Neill* [1935] IR 286; 69 ILTR 205 and *Logan v Donohue* [1938] IR 427; 73 ILTR 12 discussed at pp. 26-7 post.
5. The Emergency Powers (No. 313) Order 1944 (Amendment) Order 1945.

landlord; the Order also contained restrictions on the landlord's right to recover possession on the same lines as those in the 1923 Act.

The Rent Restrictions Act 1946 As from 12 March 1946 the Increase of Rent and Mortgage Interest (Restrictions) Act 1923, the subsequent amending Acts and the Emergency Powers Orders of 1944 and 1945 were replaced by the Rent Restrictions Act 1946.[6] By this time there were, as we have seen, two classes of controlled dwelling: those controlled under the 1923 Act whose rents were related to the rent payable in 1914, and those controlled under the 1944 Order, whose rents were related to the rent payable in 1941. The distinction between the two classes was preserved by the 1946 Act. Thus chapter 1 of part II of the Act dealt with the 'basic rent' of 'controlled (1923 Act) premises' and, generally, fixed that rent at the 'standard rent' (which bore the same meaning as it had in the 1923 Act and was thus related to the rent payable on 3 August 1914) together with an increase of twenty per cent. If the standard rent had never been determined, an application could be made to court to determine the basic rent; in such a case the basic rent was to be 'a rent of such amount as the Court considers reasonable, under any given contract of tenancy not being for more than a term of five years, having regard to the basic rents of other controlled (1923 Act) premises ...' But if there was evidence of the rent at which the premises were held on 3 August 1914, regard could be had to the amount of that rent. Chapter 2 dealt with the rent of 'controlled (non-1923 Act) premises'. In such a case the basic rent was, generally, the amount of the rent at which such premises were let on 7 May 1941, provided they were held by an occupying tenant under a contract for not more than a term of five years. Otherwise the rent was to be the amount which, in the opinion of the court, the landlord might reasonably have expected from a tenant holding under such a contract on that date. 'Lawful additions' to the basic rent were allowed where the landlord paid, or allowed a deduction, in respect of rates; expended money on the improvement or structural alteration of the premises or on repairs necessitated by acts of waste, or the neglect, of the tenant; where he otherwise spent money on putting the premises into repair; and where he was responsible, in whole or in part, for repairs. The 1946 Act unlike the earlier Acts, did not limit the amount of interest payable on mortgages. But it did continue the control of business premises, other than those let for a term of years or under a yearly tenancy, and it re-enacted the former restrictions on the landlord's right to recover possession.

The Rent Restrictions Acts 1960 and 1967 The 1946 Act remained in

6. See Coghlan, *The Law of Rent Restriction in Ireland* (Dublin, 1950), second edition.

force, subject only to minor amendments made by the Rent Restrictions (Amendment) Act 1949 and later Acts, until the commencement of the Rent Restrictions Act 1960 which was itself amended by the Rent Restrictions (Amendment) Act 1967.[7] The 1960 Act was, as O'Higgins CJ pointed out in *Blake v Attorney General* and *Madigan v Attorney General*,[8] 'the first measure dealing with rent restriction which was not expressed to be of a temporary duration'. It repealed the 1946 Act and the subsequent amending Acts, and re-enacted the existing framework of control which, at the commencement of the Act on 31 December 1960, applied to almost all privately-owned unfurnished dwellings built before 1941. But the 1960 Act did set out to decontrol some of these premises. Control was removed from purely business premises; from newly constructed separate and self-contained flats; from owner-occupied houses; and from houses with a rateable valuation exceeding £30 in Dublin or Dun Laoghaire, and £25 elsewhere, where the landlord got vacant possession. The 1967 Act extended decontrol to all houses and separate and self-contained flats where the landlord got vacant possession. The 1967 Act also decontrolled houses in Dublin and Dun Laoghaire whose rateable valuation exceeded £40 and those situate elsewhere whose rateable valuation exceeded £30; and separate and self-contained flats situate in Dublin and Dun Laoghaire whose rateable valuation exceeded £30 and those situate elsewhere whose rateable valuation exceeded £20; but the tenants of these dwellings were brought within the protection of the Landlord and Tenant Act 1931.

Under the 1960 Act the 'basic rent' was, generally, the rent at which the premises were held on 31 December 1960 less the amount of any rates paid by the landlord. Under the 1967 Act the basic rent was changed to the rent being paid on 8 June 1966, again less rates paid by the landlord. Otherwise the basic rent could be determined by the court which was bound to fix an amount which it 'considers reasonable having regard as far as possible to the basic rents of controlled dwellings which are comparable in regard to location, accommodation, amenities, state of repair and rateable valuation'. But, as was noted by O'Higgins CJ in the *Blake* and *Madigan*[9] cases, 'By reason of the provisions of earlier legislation, rents determined under (these provisions) were related to the rent which was, or might have been charged for the dwelling on 3 August 1914, or on 7 May 1941, as the case might be, subject to such flexibility as was given . . . by the words "as the court considers reasonable".' The 1960 Act allowed certain lawful additions to the basic rent, including an increase of 12.5 per cent. where the landlord was

7. See Coghlan, *The Law of Rent Restriction in the Republic of Ireland* (Dublin, 1979), third edition.
8. [1982] IR 117, 129.
9. Ibid. at pp. 129-130 of the report.

liable for repairs. Further lawful additions were allowed by the 1967 Act where the landlord expended money on maintenance of the dwelling.

The 1960 Act continued the existing restrictions on the landlord's right to recover possession, subject to certain amendments. 'The broad effect of these restrictions,' said O'Higgins CJ in *Blake* and *Madigan,*[10] 'is that a landlord cannot normally recover possession of a controlled dwelling from a tenant who pays his rent, observes the other conditions of the tenancy and does not commit nuisance or waste. Provision is, however, made for the recovery of possession by the landlord if he can establish certain special grounds. . . The restrictions contained in (the 1960 Act) may have the result that, in the absence of special grounds, possession of the dwellinghouse can never be recovered by the landlord and that possession thereof, with all the features of statutory protection, can eventually pass to different generations of the tenant's family or of the tenant's assignee.'

The *Blake* and *Madigan* cases and subsequent developments In *Blake v Attorney General* and *Madigan v Attorney General*[11] the provisions of parts II and IV of the 1960 Act were held unconstitutional. Part II contained the restrictions on the rent payable in respect of a controlled dwelling and part IV contained the restrictions on the landlord's right to recover possession. O'Higgins CJ, delivering the judgment of the court, held:[12]

> . . . the provisions of Part II of the Act of 1960 (as amended) restrict the property rights of one group of citizens for the benefit of another group. This is done without compensation and without regard to the financial capacity or the financial needs of either group, in legislation which provides no limitation on the period of restriction, gives no opportunity for review and allows no modification of the operation of the restriction. It is, therefore, both unfair and arbitrary.

As for part IV, the Chief Justice said:[13]

> It is an integral part of the arbitrary and unfair statutory scheme whereby tenants of controlled dwellings are singled out for specially favourable treatment, both as to rent and as to the right to retain possession, regardless of whether they have any social or financial need for such preferential treatment and regardless of whether the landlords have the ability to bear the burden of providing such preferential treatment.

10. Ibid. at pp. 128-9 of the report.
11. Ibid.
12. Ibid. at pp. 139-140 of the report.
13. Ibid. at p. 140 of the report.

The result of this decision was to put tenants of controlled dwellings on the same footing as other tenants: their rents fell to be determined by agreement with the landlord and their tenancies could be terminated with no restriction on the landlord's right to recover possession.

The Oireachtas responded by enacting the Rent Restrictions (Temporary Provisions) Act 1981. This Act effectively put the Supreme Court decision in abeyance pending the introduction of new legislation: it prohibited the eviction of tenants of controlled dwellings and their families and the enforcement of rent increases. The Act was due to lapse on 25 January 1982. Its provisions were extended by three months to 25 April 1982 by the Rent Restrictions (Temporary Provisions) (Continuance) Act 1981 and later to 25 July 1982 by the Rent Restrictions (Temporary Provisions) (Continuance) Act 1982. The Government in the meantime submitted new legislation, the Housing (Private Rented Dwellings) Bill, 1981, to the Oireachtas. This Bill was passed by both houses and was subsequently referred to the Supreme Court by the President under article 26 of the Constitution. The Supreme Court in *In re Reference under article 26 of the Constitution of the Housing (Private Rented Dwellings) Bill, 1981*[14] held that provisions in the 1981 Bill allowing rebates in favour of tenants on the rents payable by them for a period of five years were unconstitutional, constituting an unjust attack on the property rights of landlords of controlled dwellings.

The Housing (Private Rented Dwellings) Acts 1982 and 1983 A new Bill was then initiated and ultimately enacted as the Housing (Private Rented Dwellings) Act 1982. The Act was brought into operation by ministerial order[15] on 26 July 1982. It is this Act which now forms the basis of control over private rented dwellings. It grants a measure of security of tenure to the tenants of dwellings which were controlled under the 1960 and 1967 Acts and provided for the fixing of the terms of the tenancies by the District Court. The 1982 Act was, however, amended by the Housing (Private Rented Dwellings) (Amendment) Act 1983 which was brought into force on 2 August 1983.[16] This Act provides that the terms of tenancies are to be fixed by a new body known as the Rent Tribunal.

14. [1983] IR 181; [1983] ILRM 246.
15. Housing (Private Rented Dwellings) Act 1982 (Commencement) Order 1982, SI No. 216 of 1982.
16. Housing (Private Rented Dwellings) (Amendment) Act 1983 (Commencement) Order 1983, SI No. 221 of 1983.

TWO

Controlled dwellings

Control under the 1982 and 1983 Acts Control of tenancies is now regulated by Part II of the Housing (Private Rented Dwellings) Act 1982 as amended by the Housing (Private Rented Dwellings) (Amendment) Act 1983. Part II applies to every dwelling which at the commencement of the Act was a controlled dwelling within the meaning of the Rent Restrictions Acts, 1960 to 1981 other than a dwelling held under a contract of tenancy for longer than from year to year.[1] So, although the 1982 Act repeals the 1960 and 1967 Rent Restrictions Acts, these Acts cannot be forgotten: their provisions are still relevant when deciding whether a dwelling is controlled. This point was taken by Costello J in *Foley v Johnson*[2] which concerned licensed premises with living accommodation overhead. The tenant argued that, because of the business user, the premises were not a dwelling within the special meaning of that word laid down in section 2 of the 1982 Act and that therefore the premises were not controlled. Costello J held,[3] however, that in order to determine whether premises are controlled 'the inquirer (has) to consider whether the premises would have been regarded as a "controlled dwelling within the meaning of the Rent Restrictions Acts, 1960 to 1981", and not whether they come within the statutory definition of dwelling in the 1982 Act.'

Only dwellings are protected The Housing (Private Rented Dwellings) Act 1982 as amended by the Housing (Private Rented Dwellings) (Amendment) Act 1983 protects dwellings. A 'dwelling' is defined in section 2(1) of the 1982 Act as 'a house let as a separate dwelling, or a part so let, of any house, whether or not the tenant shares with any other persons any portion thereof or any accommodation, amenity or facility in connection therewith.' A police barracks has been held not to be a premises let as a dwelling even though some of the police stationed in it lived and slept there.[4]

1. Housing (Private Rented Dwellings) Act 1982, section 8(1).
2. [1988] IR 7.
3. At p. 9 of the report.
4. *Martin Estates Company Ltd v Watt* [1925] NI 79.

The requirement that there be a letting For the Acts to apply there must be a letting. But if the letting is for a period greater than from year to year, the dwelling is not controlled.[5] Because there is no letting, neither a trespasser nor a licensee can claim the protection of the Acts. Nor can a tenant at will claim protection.[6] A dwelling let bona fide for temporary convenience or to a person in connection with his continuance in any office, appointment or employment is also outside the Acts for the purposes of the tenant's right to retain possession and recovery of possession by the landlord.[7]

The letting of a separate dwelling To come within the Acts the dwelling must be let as a separate dwelling. In *Bradley v McGowan*[8] premises consisting of a large site, which the tenant used as a builder's yard and in which he claimed to reside, were held not to have been let as a separate dwelling. A dwelling may, however, be within the Acts even if it is used in part for business purposes.[9] Thus in *Burns v Radcliffe*[10] premises were held to be controlled where they had been let to the tenant for use as an hotel and he resided there. But though a tenant may use his dwelling in part for business purposes and continue to claim the protection of the Acts, he cannot, it seems, claim that the premises are, in addition, 'business premises' and so attract the right to a new tenancy under the Landlord and Tenant (Amendment) Act 1980.[11]

No control where the rateable valuation exceeds certain limits A dwelling is not controlled where its rateable valuation exceeds the prescribed limit.[12] Thus a separate and self-contained flat situate in the county borough of Dublin or the borough of Dun Laoghaire is not controlled if the rateable valuation exceeds £30. A separate and self-contained flat situate elsewhere is not controlled if the rateable valuation exceeds £20. A house situate in the county borough of Dublin or the borough of Dun Laoghaire is not controlled if the rateable valuation exceeds £40. A house situate elsewhere is not

5. Housing (Private Rented Dwellings) Act 1982, section 8(1).
6. *Delany (Blanchardstown Mills Ltd) v Jones* [1938] IR 826 followed in *Irish Sailors' and Soldiers' Land Trust v Donnelly* [1944] IR 464; 78 ILTR 113.
7. Housing (Private Rented Dwellings) Act 1982, section 8(2) and see below pp. 17-21.
8. [1951] IR 72.
9. Section 8(1) of the Housing (Private Rented Dwellings) Act 1982 and section 4 of the Rent Restrictions Act 1960. See also *Mullane v Brosnan* [1974] IR 222 and *Foley v Johnson*, supra.
10. [1923] 2 IR 158. See also *Plunkett v Lenehan* 62 ILTR 29.
11. *Mullane v Brosnan* [1974] IR 222. See also *Daly v Love* 79 ILTR 71 where it was held that a tenant who applied for a new tenancy under the Landlord and Tenant Act could not also avail of the protection of the Rent Act.
12. Rent Restrictions Act 1960, section 3(2)(a) as amended by Rent Restrictions (Amendment) Act 1967, section 2(1).

controlled if the rateable valuation exceeds £30. A dwelling which is neither a house nor a separate and self-contained flat situate in the county borough of Dublin or the borough of Dun Laoghaire is not controlled if the rateable valuation exceeds £60. A dwelling which is neither a house nor a separate and self-contained flat, and is situate elsewhere, is not controlled if the rateable valuation exceeds £40. Dwellings which were decontrolled by reason of the changes in the valuation limits effected by the Rent Restrictions (Amendment) Act 1967 are now subject to the Landlord and Tenant Act provided the letting was not made for temporary convenience or dependent on the continuance in any office, employment or appointment.[13]

Where the rateable valuation of a dwelling is increased and, as a result, exceeds the limit for control, the dwelling continues to be controlled unless and until the landlord comes into possession.[14] Possession here means actual possession, and a landlord is not deemed to have come into possession by reason only of a change of tenancy made with his consent.[15]

No control were the dwelling was erected on or after 7 May 1941 A dwelling is not controlled if it was erected after 7 May 1941.[16] Nor is it controlled if it was in the course of erection on that date. The cases[17] show that for a dwelling to have been erected after the critical date it is not necessary for it to have been built entirely from scratch on an empty site. The dwelling will be held to have erected where use is made of the shell of a former building. Thus in *McDonagh v Mulholland*[18] the premises when originally built as a house at some time prior to 1919 contained four rooms plus a small hall and outside water closet. In 1952 the building was largely reconstructed, the ground floor kitchen being converted into a shop and a shop window inserted. A new kitchen and a bathroom were built at the rere of the premises. One of the upstairs rooms was partitioned, the entire roof completely renewed and the walls partly rebuilt. The gable walls of the house were not altered. It was held that the premises had been erected since 1941. A court may hold a dwelling to have been erected where premises, which were formerly used for other purposes, are converted into residential accommodation. In *Somers v Hutchinson*[19] the landlord purchased a dwellinghouse

13. Landlord and Tenant (Amendment) Act 1980, section 15.
14. Rent Restrictions Act 1960, section 3(4) as amended by Rent Restrictions (Amendment) Act 1967, section 2(1).
15. Ibid., section 3(7) as amended by Rent Restrictions (Amendment) Act 1967, section 2(5).
16. Ibid., section 3(2)(b).
17. See *Casserley v Graham* 63 ILTR 162; *Keeler v Brangan* 64 ILTR 213; *Barry v McTighe* [1940] Ir Jur Rep 26.
18. [1957] Ir Jur Rep 4.
19. 64 ILTR 103.

which was situated over a shed. He converted the shed into living quarters and put in a staircase to connect them to the rooms upstairs. The entire dwellinghouse was let to the tenant. Again it was held that the dwellinghouse had been erected after the critical date.[20]

No control of dwellings let by local authorities Lettings by local authorities are excluded from control by section 3(2)(c) of the 1960 Act which provides that a dwelling let under the Labourers Acts 1883 to 1958 or the Housing of the Working Classes Acts 1890 to 1958 is not controlled. Dwellings let under these Acts are now deemed to be let under the Housing Act.[21] The Housing Act also prohibits reliance on the 1960 Act as a defence to a claim for possession where a repairs notice, closing order or demolition order has been made in respect of premises.[22] Nor can the 1960 Act be relied upon where a housing authority seeks a warrant for possession of a dwellinghouse or building under section 62 of the Housing Act.[23] Similarly the Local Government (Planning and Development) Act 1963 excludes the application of the 1960 Act to a lease granted by a planning authority under section 75 of that Act.[24]

No control of furnished lettings A dwelling which is let fully furnished is prevented by section 3(2)(d) of the 1960 Act from being controlled. This subsection provides that a dwelling is not controlled if the reserved rent:

> includes payments for board, attendance or the use of furniture, or for the supply to the dwelling of heat, hot water, fuel, electricity or any other commodity or for the rendering of any services in connection with the dwelling, unless, on apportionment of the reserved rent by the Court, the portion of the reserved rent which, in the opinion of the Court, is attributable to the dwelling alone equals or exceeds three quarters of the reserved rent . . .

In simpler terms, a furnished dwelling is not controlled unless the amount of the rent attributable to the dwelling alone equals or exceeds three quarters of the total rent.

The correct method for determining whether or not the portion of the rent attributable to the dwelling alone equals or exceeds three quarters of the reserved rent was laid down in *Hanratty v Hardy*.[25] There Davitt J expressly

20. See also *Sweeney v O'Sheaghdha* 72 ILTR 255.
21. Housing Act 1966, section 118(1).
22. Ibid., section 66(17).
23. Ibid., section 62(6).
24. Local Government (Planning and Development) Act 1963, section 75(4)(b).
25. [1947] Ir Jur Rep 42.

approved the method suggested by counsel that one must:

> determine, from the evidence of valuers or otherwise, the fair letting value of the premises unfurnished and the fair letting value of the same premises with such furniture as has actually been supplied, and then divide the reserved rent in the proportion which those two hypothetical figures bear to each other. Unless on such a division the proportion attributable to an unfurnished letting of the premises is equal to or exceeds three quarters of the whole, the premises are not within the protection of the Act.

In the course of his judgment Davitt J said that he thought it was the intention of the 1946 Rent Act to exclude fully furnished lettings from its protection. Subsequently in *Little v Davies*[26] Haugh J said that he took the 'view of Davitt J, expressed in *Hanratty v Hardy*, that a fully furnished letting is not protected by . . . the Act . . .' This interpretation placed by Haugh J on the words of Davitt J in *Hanratty v Hardy*[27] may be misleading in so far as it suggests a rule that a fully furnished letting must be outside the scope of the Acts. The true test is the one laid down in section 3(2)(d) of the 1960 Act. In *Murphy v Kenny*[28] Davitt J explained his decision in *Hanratty* thus:

> I am still of the opinion that it is the intention of the Act that genuinely fully furnished lettings should be excluded. The crux is, of course, what is a fully furnished letting? The only test which the Act provides and allows is the test of apportionment. If on such apportionment over three-fourths of the rent is attributable to the dwelling-house alone, then the premises are within the Act.

The Supreme Court has held, in *Parkinson v O'Malley*,[29] that it is open to the court to ignore the apportionment of the rent between the dwelling and the furniture made by the parties and to make its own apportionment. And it seems that the apportionment of the rent may be made as of the date of the court proceedings. This follows from *Fridberg v Doyle*[30] where the landlord sought possession of a furnished flat in which some of the furnishings had worn out. Although the flat was evidently not controlled when initially let, it was held to be controlled when ejectment proceedings were brought in the Circuit Court.

26. [1949] Ir Jur Rep 24, 25.
27. Supra.
28. [1950] Ir Jur Rep 1, 2.
29. [1940] IR 498.
30. [1981] ILRM 370. Cf. *Palser v Grinling* [1948] AC 291.

The meaning of 'furniture' was discussed at length by Viscount Simon in *Palser v Grinling*.[31] He said that because 'furniture' has a statutory meaning, that meaning cannot be extended merely because the lease provides that certain things are to be regarded as 'furniture'; 'furniture' cannot include anything which is already paid for by the portion of the rent attributable to the dwelling itself; and only those articles which are currently and commonly regarded as furniture can rank as such. The services referred to in section 3(2)(d) are services rendered by the landlord. Where services were rendered by the tenant in return for a reduction in the rent, they were disregarded and the premises were held to be controlled.[32]

No control where a house is occupied by its owner on or after 31 December 1960 A house is not controlled if it was occupied by its owner on or after 31 December 1960 for the purposes of his own residence.[33] The term 'owner' includes any person having any estate or interest in the house other than under a contract of tenancy for a term of twenty-one years or less.[34] The 1967 Act provides that a house will not be decontrolled by reason only of the fact that it is owner occupied on or after 31 December 1960 where on 9 May 1967 it is occupied for the purposes of his own residence by a person who holds it under a lease for a term of more than twenty-one years.[35] But if neither the person who holds the house under a lease for more than twenty-one years nor any other person having the lessee's interest under the lease occupies the house for the purposes of his own residence before the expiration of the term, the house ceases to be controlled.[36] The effect of the 1967 amendment was to reapply control to the house occupied by the lessee under a long lease so long as he remained in occupation; but to allow for decontrol when he ceased to be in occupation.

No control of a house over certain rateable valuation limits where the landlord is in possession on or after 31 December 1960; and no control of any house where the landlord comes into possession on or after 8 June 1966 A house of which the landlord is in possession on 31 December 1960, or comes into possession thereafter, is not controlled if the rateable valuation exceeds £30 and the house is situate in the county borough of Dublin or the borough of Dun Laoghaire, or if the rateable valuation exceeds £25 and the house is situate elsewhere.[37] Where the landlord comes into possession on

31. [1948] AC 291.
32. *Elkinson v Cassidy* 110 ILTR 27.
33. Rent Restrictions Act 1960, section 3(2)(e).
34. Ibid., section 3(6).
35. Rent Restrictions (Amendment) Act 1967, section 2(6).
36. Ibid.
37. Rent Restrictions Act 1960, section 3(2)(f).

or after 8 June 1966 the requirement as to rateable valuation does not apply.[38] 'Possession' means actual possession, and a landlord is not deemed to have come into possession by reason only of a change of tenancy made with his consent.[39]

The question of decontrol by the landlord's possession was considered by the Supreme Court in *Griffin v Kennedy*.[40] Here there was a change of tenancy and the landlord did extensive repairs and renovations before the new tenants went into occupation. It was held that the landlord had not come into possession so as to decontrol the premises. Henchy J said[41] that:

> In that point of time which elapses between one tenancy ending and the tenancy to follow straight away there is a slight break, but that is not sufficient to give the landlord actual possession of the premises. The legislature envisaged something more being required. What is required is a *de facto* physical relationship.

No control of certain separate and self-contained flats A separate and self-contained flat forming part of buildings which, after 31 December 1960, were reconstructed by way of conversion into two or more separate and self-contained flats is not controlled.[42] A separate and self-contained flat not forming part of such buildings, and of which the landlord is in possession on or after 8 June 1966, is also not controlled.[43] Again 'possession' means actual possession.[44]

What is a separate and self-contained flat? A flat is 'separate' where it forms a distinct unit. To be 'separate and self-contained' a flat does not have to lie entirely within one ambit; in other words, not all the rooms must lie behind one door. Thus it was held in *O'Sullivan v Cullen*[45] that the fact that the tenant had to pass along some twelve steps which formed part of the common user of the house when going from her kitchenette to her dining-room did not prevent the flat from being separate and self-contained. Likewise in *Broadhead v Knox*[46] a flat comprising rooms on the two top floors

38. Section 3(2)(f) as amended by Rent Restrictions (Amendment) Act 1967, section 2(2).
39. Rent Restrictions Act 1960, section 3(7) as amended by Rent Restrictions (Amendment) Act 1967, section 2(5).
40. 99 ILTR 199.
41. Ibid. at p. 202.
42. Rent Restrictions Act 1960, section 3(2)(g).
43. Ibid., section 3(2)(g) as amended by Rent Restrictions (Amendment) Act 1967, section 2(3).
44. Ibid., section 3(7) as amended by Rent Restrictions (Amendment) Act 1967, section 2(5) and see *Griffin v Kennedy*, supra.
45. 59 ILTR 133.
46. 109 ILTR 116.

of a house and a lavatory on the half floor, which was visible from the lower floor which comprised another tenancy, was held to be separate and self-contained. But where the toilet was used in common with the tenants of other flats it was held in *Elkinson v Cassidy*[47] that the flat was not self-contained, even though the letting agreement referred to it as being 'self-contained'.

What amounts to reconstruction by way of conversion? Hanna J in *Boyle v Fitzsimons*[48] pointed out that: 'While reconstruction may literally mean constructing again, its connotation would fairly cover something substantial or radical done anew, or in the nature of fresh construction.' In *Noyk v O'Brien*[49] reconstruction was said to be a matter of degree. There substantial improvements had been made including the provision of new bathrooms and lavatories, the replacement of old fireplaces, the removal of old sinks, the plastering of walls and the installation of new flooring. These works, it was held, were not a sufficient reconstruction. Nor, it was held in *McCann v Cotter*,[50] did the provision of water and gas constitute reconstruction. To determine whether there is a reconstruction, a court will have regard to the objects of the work and the result obtained.[51] Another factor will be the cost. But even where the expenditure on repairs was substantial, the court has refused to hold that there was a reconstruction.[52]

Where there is a reconstruction affecting only part of a dwelling, the unaffected part may remain controlled.[53] But, in another case, the District Court has held that the part unaffected by the reconstruction was decontrolled.[54]

No control of a dwelling let with land where the rateable valuation of the land exceeds a certain limit A dwelling let with land other than the site of the dwelling is not controlled, provided the rateable valuation of the land exceeds the lesser of the following: half the rateable valuation of the site including the building or buildings on it; or £10 where the dwelling is situate in the county borough of Dublin or the borough of Dun Laoghaire, and £5 in any other case.[55] The effect of this provision is to exclude from control

47. 110 ILTR 27.
48. [1926] IR 378, 382-3.
49. 76 ILTR 66.
50. 59 ILTR 113.
51. *O'Sullivan v Cullen* 59 ILTR 133.
52. *Gore-Grimes v Foley* 64 ILTR 52.
53. *Connolly v Gleeson* [1942] IR 68; 75 ILTR 227.
54. *Downes v Kennedy* 110 ILTR 25.
55. Rent Restrictions Act 1960, section 3(2)(h). Under sections 41 and 49 of the 1960 Act the Commissioner of Valuation and the court were empowered to apportion the rateable valuation of a property. However, these sections were repealed by section 6 of the 1982 Act and no similar provisions have since been re-enacted.

dwellings let with any substantial amount of land. To determine whether a dwelling let with land is controlled one is required to ascertain the rateable valuation of the land and the rateable valuation of the site on which the dwelling is located. The latter figure must include any buildings on the site. One must then compare the figure for half the rateable valuation of the site with the figure of £10 where the dwelling is situate in Dublin or Dun Laoghaire or £5 where the dwelling is situate elsewhere. Taking the lesser figure of these, one compares this figure with the rateable valuation of the land. If the rateable valuation of the land is greater, control is excluded.

The meaning of the phrase 'the site of the dwelling' was considered by the Supreme Court in *O'Reilly v Wesley Acres*.[56] It was held that the phrase refers to that part of the land upon which the dwelling and its out-offices stand, as distinct from adjoining land comprised in the same letting. However, in an older case, *Wills v McGrane*,[57] Judge Shannon in the Circuit Court held that the word 'site' meant only the actual portion of the land upon which the four walls of the house stood. According to Murnaghan J in *Mason v Leavy*,[58] 'It is a question of practical judgment how much unbuilt-on land is part of the house.'

Where prior to 31 December 1960, a dwelling stood let with land other than its site and the Rent Restrictions Act 1946 applied to the dwelling, it remains controlled unless and until the landlord comes into possession.[59] This is so even if the dwelling may not be controlled under section 3(2)(h) of the 1960 Act.[60]

No control of a house, the rateable valuation of which exceeds £10, which becomes tenanted by a bachelor or spinster over 21 and under 65 after 9 May 1967 A house is not controlled if its rateable valuation exceeds £10 and a bachelor or spinster over the age of 21 and under the age of 65 has become the tenant after 9 May 1967.[61] A tenant whose house has been decontrolled in these circumstances may, however, claim a new tenancy under the Landlord and Tenant Act.[62]

Service lettings Sections 9 and 16 of the 1982 Act relating to the right to retain possession and the recovery of possession of a controlled dwelling do

56. [1974] IR 454.
57. 65 ILTR 86.
58. [1952] IR 40, 48; 88 ILTR 61.
59. Rent Restrictions Act 1960, section 3(5).
60. Ibid.
61. Ibid., section 3(2) as amended by Rent Restrictions (Amendment) Act 1967 section 2(4).
62. Landlord and Tenant (Amendment) Act 1980, section 15(2).

not apply to a dwelling subject to a service letting.[63] Similar provision was made in relation to service lettings under the old legislation.[64] It will be noted that the dwelling must be let to the tenant 'in connection with his continuance in any office, appointment or employment'. So, if the landlord has allowed the tenant to remain in possession of the dwelling after the service or employment has ended and has accepted rent from him, then the full force of the Act may apply. For example, in *Great Northern Railway Company (Ireland) v Best*,[65] the plaintiff company let a house to the defendant under a written agreement which provided that the tenancy was to terminate when the defendant ceased to be in the employment of the company. After the defendant's employment ceased, he continued to occupy the house at the same rent as before. When the plaintiff company sought possession it was held that the tenancy which had been created by the written agreement had terminated when the employment ceased, and that the second letting was not made in consideration of the tenant's employment. That decision should, however, be contrasted with the decision in *Great Southern Railways v Bergin*.[66] Here the widow of a deceased employee remained in occupation after the death of her husband of a cottage held by him for the duration of his employment. She paid the same weekly sum for rent as had been deducted from her husband's wages by way of rent. After two months she signed an acknowledgment that she had been permitted to occupy the house for temporary convenience only. Some time later the employers served notice to quit and commenced ejectment proceedings. It was held that the acceptance of rent for two months was not, in the circumstances, sufficient evidence of a new tenancy, and that the employers were entitled to permit the widow of their deceased employee to remain in occupation for a reasonable time without a new tenancy being created.

Temporary convenience lettings Sections 9 and 16 of the 1982 Act also do not apply to dwelling let bona fide for temporary convenience or to meet a temporary necessity.[67] Again similar provision was made in the old legislation.[68] The exclusion of temporary convenience lettings from the rigours of control has given rise to much litigation in the past. The reason for this was perhaps suggested by Fitzgibbon LJ in *McCutcheon v Wilson*[69] when he said this about temporary convenience:

63. Housing (Private Rented Dwellings) Act 1982, section 8(2)(a).
64. See Rent Restrictions Act 1960, section 37.
65. 55 ILTR 57.
66. 71 ILTR 276.
67. Housing (Private Rented Dwellings) Act 1982, section 8(2)(b).
68. See Rent Restrictions Act 1960, section 37.
69. Unreported, but quoted with approval by Palles CB in *Driscoll v Riordan* 16 LR Ir 235, 244.

> Every letting is in a sense for the convenience or to meet a necessity of one or other or both of the parties; but the temporary convenience or necessity contemplated here must, I think, be something special, peculiar to the party or parties or to the holding, collateral to, or possibly even irrespective of the quantity or quality of the tenant's interest, not expected to continue to exist at another time or in other hands, and must be shown to have formed the motive of the letting at the time.

The purpose of the letting was emphasised by Gibson J in *Herron v O'Donnell*[70] when he pointed out that:

> the question as to whether a letting was for the temporary convenience or to meet the temporary necessity of either the landlord or tenant depends on the object or motive of the letting, and not on its legal duration.

However, it has been held that it is open to a landlord to make a letting for temporary convenience for one reason and to seek possession for a different reason.[71]

A consideration of the reported cases shows that the courts have been willing to hold that lettings were made for temporary convenience or to meet a temporary necessity where there is evidence to support this conclusion. But if the evidence does not admit the inference of a temporary convenience letting, the courts have refused to hold that the letting was of a temporary nature even where the letting agreement expressly states that it is for temporary convenience only. Thus in *Carton v McManus*[72] the letting agreement recited that it was for temporary convenience, but the evidence disclosed that at the date of the letting there was no temporary convenience either of the plaintiff or of the defendant. It was held that the mere statement of temporary convenience was not enough: there had to be actual temporary convenience. Furthermore, although a letting may initially be for temporary convenience, if the tenant is allowed to remain in occupation beyond the period of temporary convenience, the letting will lose its temporary character. So in *Murphy v O'Connell*[73] it was held that a letting of a controlled premises for a period of not more than 18 months made for the temporary convenience of the tenant had, by reason of the tenant having been permitted to remain on for a further period of 19 months without being requested to vacate the premises, ceased to be a letting for the temporary convenience or

70. 42 ILTR 227, 228.
71. *Fitzpatrick v Hoey* 89 ILT & SJ 168.
72. 96 ILT & SJ 92. See also *Moynihan v O'Sullivan* 87 ILT & SJ 118.
73. [1949] Ir Jur Rep 1.

to meet the temporary necessity of the tenant within the provisions of the 1946 Rent Act.

The nature of the temporary convenience or necessity has, in some of the reported cases, been clear. For example, in *Stokes v Moloney*,[74] the letting was held to be one of temporary convenience where the dwelling was let to a bank official until such time as he should be moved on to some other town. In *Flood v Smith*[75] the landlord took temporary work in England and let his Dublin residence on a monthly tenancy. The tenancy agreement did not, however, refer to the reason or the temporary nature of the letting. After he had returned to Dublin it was held that the landlord was entitled to a decree for possession, the letting having been made to meet his temporary necessity. In *Kaye v Kelly*[76] the landlord let rooms in his house in order to raise money to make repayments to a superannuation fund. It was held that the letting had been made to meet a temporary necessity; but Dixon J expressed the view that, if the letting had merely been made out of a desire to supplement a small income, he might have come to a different conclusion.

In other cases it is less easy to see the temporary convenience. For example, in *Macbeth v Bishopp*,[77] the landlord let a furnished dwelling to the tenant for one year with an option to renew for a further year. No formal renewal was ever granted but the tenancy in fact lasted nearly four years. The landlord instituted ejectment proceedings and the tenant relied on the 1946 Rent Act. Although the letting agreement did not indicate that the letting had been made for the temporary convenience or to meet a temporary necessity of either party, it was held that the letting had been made for the temporary convenience of both parties. In *Rinn v McCarthy*[78] the tenant signed an agreement to take the landlord's house for a period of six months while the landlord expected to be in America. The purpose of the letting was explained to the tenant but was not expressed in the agreement. On the expiration of the six months two further agreements for six months each were signed by the tenant. Thereafter, for four periods of six months each, similar agreements were sent to the tenant; he did not sign or return them but did pay the rent due. On the expiration of the last of these periods the landlord brought an action to recover possession. The Supreme Court held that the letting had been made for the temporary convenience or temporary necessity of the landlord and that he was entitled to possession. In *Bank of Ireland v Lyons*[79] part of a house had been let to a nursing home for use as a nurses' hostel, the

74. [1959] Ir Jur Rep 57.
75. [1946] IR 130.
76. [1948] IR 383.
77. [1948] Ir Jur Rep 49.
78. [1925] 2 IR 157.
79. [1951] Ir Jur Rep 3.

landlord undertaking to prepare meals for the nurses, to keep the premises cleaned and to perform certain other duties. The landlord's successor subsequently let the remainder of the house to another tenant in consideration of the payment of a weekly rent and the performance by the tenant of all the services which the successor was bound by the first letting to perform. On the termination of the letting to the nursing home, the plaintiffs, as the persons then entitled to the landlord's interest in the entire house, sought to obtain possession of the premises comprised in the second letting. This letting, it was held, had been made for the temporary convenience or to meet a temporary necessity of the landlord and a decree for possession was granted.

Where a letting has been made by a trustee, or on behalf of an infant, the courts have been prepared to hold that it was for temporary convenience. So in *O'Connor v Heylin*[80] a letting agreement, expressed to be for the temporary convenience of the landlord, was entered into by the plaintiff landlord's mother in her capacity as trustee for the plaintiff. In an action for ejectment it was held that the plaintiff was entitled to rely on the temporary convenience clause. And in *Fitzgerald v Broderick*[81] a letting was made for the duration of the infancy of the landlord who, on coming of age, allowed the tenant to remain on for as long as four years. The initial temporary convenience, it was held, did not come to an end on the landlord's attaining full age.

Dwellings let by the state It is not clear whether dwellings let by the Commissioners of Public Works, the Land Commission or a government minister come within the 1982 Act. The older cases suggest that the Rent Acts did not apply to the state. The leading case was *Cork County Council and another v Commissioners of Public Works and others*[82] in which the Supreme Court held that the Commissioners of Public Works were not bound by the provisions of the 1923 Rent Act. O'Byrne J quoted with approval from the judgment of Story J in *United States v Hoar*[83] who had said that it is 'a safe rule, founded in the principles of the Common Law, that the general words of a statute ought not to include the Government, or affect its rights, unless that construction be clear and indisputable upon the text of the Act'. But the exclusion of the state from the application of its own enactments has historically been based on a prerogative right of the crown[84] to which, it was assumed, the state succeeded. The validity of this assumption was first questioned by Walsh J in *Byrne v Ireland*[85] when he pointed out that crown

80. 83 ILTR 79.
81. Unreported, but referred to at 84 ILT & SJ 243.
82. [1945] IR 561.
83. (1821) 26 Fed Cas 329.
84. See Kelly, *The Irish Constitution* (Dublin, 1984), second edition, pp. 695- 699 and Casey, *Constitutional Law in Ireland* (London, 1987), pp. 59-61.
85. [1972] IR 241.

prerogatives were based on the notion that the king was the personification of the state and that he could 'do no wrong'. These ideas, though, he held to be inconsistent not just with the provisions of the present Constitution, but also the Constitution of the Irish Free State. 'All royal prerogatives,' he said,[86] 'to be found in the common law of England and in the common law of Ireland prior to the enactment of the Constitution of Saorstát Éireann, 1922, ceased to be part of the law of Saorstát Éireann because they were based on concepts expressly repudiated by . . . that Constitution and, therefore, were inconsistent with the provisions of that Constitution and were not carried over by Article 73 thereof (providing for the continuance of laws in force).' Referring to the provisions of the present Constitution, Walsh J said,[87] 'In my view, the whole tenor of our Constitution is to the effect that there is no power, institution or person in the land free of the law save where such immunity is expressed, or provided for, in the Constitution itself'.

The status of the royal prerogative was reconsidered in *Webb v Ireland*[88] which arose out of the discovery by the plaintiffs, using metal detectors, of the Derrynaflan hoard. The state, in resisting the plaintiffs' claim for the return of the hoard, claimed that it was treasure trove. Treasure trove is, however, a prerogative right; and so the question arose whether this right had survived the decision in *Byrne v Ireland*. The Supreme Court held that it had not; Finlay CJ, with whose judgment Henchy and Griffin JJ agreed, said[89]

> I agree with the view reached by the learned trial judge in this case that on the authority of *Byrne v Ireland* . . . no royal prerogative in existence prior to the enactment of the Constitution of 1922 was by virtue of the provisions of that Constitution vested in the Irish Free State. . . As is also set out in the decision in *Byrne v Ireland*, it must follow from this conclusion that the royal prerogatives were not prerogatives exercisable in Saorstát Éireann immediately before 11 December, 1936, and were therefore not captured by Article 49, s.1 of the (1937) Constitution (declaring that prerogatives belong to the people).

Finlay CJ did, however, go on to hold that a right or prerogative of treasure trove does exist, but only as 'an inherent attribute of the sovereignty of the State'.[90]

86. At pp. 274-5 of the report.
87. At p. 281 of the report.
88. [1988] IR 353; [1988] ILRM 565.
89. At p. 382 of the report.
90. At p. 383 of the report. The basis for this particular right was found in articles 5 and 10 of the Constitution, the former with its express description of the state as 'sovereign', and the latter with its assertion that 'All natural resources . . . within the jurisdiction of the Parliament and Government established by this Constitution and all royalties and franchises within that jurisdiction belong to the State.'

It follows that, although no purely royal prerogative survives today as part of our law, rights in the nature of prerogative rights may exist where there is some basis for them in the provisions of the Constitution; and a case could conceivably be made for a right in favour of the state excluding it from the application of its own legislation. But authority suggests that such an exclusion can only be justified where there is a rational basis for it;[91] and it is difficult to see a rational basis for the exclusion of the state from the application of the Housing (Private Rented Dwellings) Act. The position of the state under the Landlord and Tenant (Amendment) Act 1980 provides an interesting contrast. Section 4 of that Act provides that, save where a state authority acquires the interest of the lessor after the commencement of the Act 'this Act shall not bind a State authority in its capacity as lessor or immediate lessor of any premises.' The 1982 Act enacted after the Landlord and Tenant Act does not contain a similar exclusion. This absence of an exclusion must lend weight to the argument that the legislature intended to bind the state under the 1982 Act.

91. See the comments of Walsh J on the *Cork County Council* case and *United States v Hoar* at pp. 275-6 and 278 of *Byrne v Ireland*, supra.

THREE

Decontrol, recontrol and the application of the Landlord and Tenant Act to formerly controlled properties

Cessation of control under the 1982 Act The protection afforded by part II of the 1982 Act ceases in any one of the three circumstances set out in section 8(3). They are: (1) where the tenant's entitlement to possession ceases to subsist; (2) where the tenant assigns or sublets his tenancy; and (3) where the landlord recovers possession of the dwelling.

Cessation of control under the old legislation As we have already seen, the 1982 Act applies to dwellings which were formerly controlled other than those held under a contract of tenancy for greater than from year to year.[1] Consequently, dwellings which ceased to be controlled under the old legislation are not protected under the 1982 Act. Decontrol could be brought about in two ways under the old legislation: by a change in the legislative criteria for control or, in certain cases, by the landlord's coming into possession. A change in the legislative criteria was, for example, effected by section 2(1) of the 1967 Rent Restrictions (Amendment) Act which amended section 3(2)(a) of the 1960 Act. Under section 3(2)(a) a dwelling in Dublin or Dun Laoghaire was not controlled if its rateable valuation exceeded £60; and a dwelling was not controlled, if situate elsewhere, if its rateable valuation exceeded £40. Section 2(1) of the 1967 Act decontrolled dwellings by providing that houses and separate and self-contained flats situate in Dublin and Dun Laoghaire were not controlled if the rateable valuation exceeded £40 and £30 respectively; and houses and separate and self-contained flats situate elsewhere were freed from control if their rateable valuations exceeded £30 and £20 respectively. The 1960 and 1967 Acts also provided for decontrol on the occurrence of some event, usually on a landlord or owner's

1. Housing (Private Rented Dwellings) Act 1982, section 8 (1).

coming into possession. The following is a summary of these decontrolling provisions:

— a house occupied by its owner as his own residence on or after the commencement of the 1960 Act (31 December 1960): 1960 Act, section 3(2)(e) and 3(6) and the 1967 Act, section 2(6);

— a house of which the landlord comes into possession on or after 8 June 1966: 1960 Act, section 3(2)(f) as amended by the 1967 Act, section 2(2);

— a house of which the landlord is in possession or comes into possession on or after the commencement of the 1960 Act (31 December 1960) provided the rateable valuation exceeds £30 if the house is situate in Dublin or Dun Laoghaire or £25 if the house is situate elsewhere: 1960 Act, section 3(2)(f) as amended by the 1967 Act, section 2(2);

— a separate and self-contained flat forming part of buildings which, after the commencement of the 1960 Act (31 December 1960), were reconstructed by way of conversion into two or more separate and self-contained flats: 1960 Act, section 3(2)(g) as amended by the 1967 Act, section 2(3);

— a separate and self-contained flat, which does not form part of buildings reconstructed by way of conversion into two or more separate and self-contained flats after the commencement of the 1960 Act (31 December 1960), of which the landlord is in possession on 8 June 1966 or comes into possession thereafter: 1960 Act, section 3(2)(g) as amended by the 1967 Act, section 2(3);

— a dwelling the rateable valuation of which is increased beyond the limits for control and of which the landlord comes into possession: 1960 Act, section 3(4) as amended by the 1967 Act, section 2(1);

— a dwelling let with land other than the site of the dwelling to which the Rent Restrictions Act 1946 applied of which the landlord comes into possession: 1960 Act, section 3(5);

— a house the rateable valuation of which exceeds £10 which becomes tenanted by a bachelor or spinster over 21 and under 65 after the passing of the 1967 Act (9 May 1967): 1960 Act, section 3(2) as amended by the 1967 Act, section 2(4).

Recontrol The possibility that a decontrolled dwelling might once again become subject to the Rent Acts is effectively excluded by section 9(1) of the 1982 Act which limits the entitlement to retain possession to the original tenant, that is to say, the tenant at the commencement of the Act and his relations. Consequently, a landlord who gains possession of a controlled dwelling after the commencement of the 1982 Act need not fear the possibility of recontrol. It seems doubtful, moreover, that recontrol was possible under the old legislation. It was decided by the Supreme Court in *Donnelly v O'Neill*[2] that, where a dwelling had been decontrolled, a subsequent letting of part of the dwelling could not be controlled. In that case the landlord had got vacant possession of a dwellinghouse which had formerly been let as a controlled dwelling. The dwelling ceased to be controlled under section 5(1) of the 1926 Rent Act. This subsection excluded the application of the 1923 Rent Act from a dwellinghouse to which the Act otherwise applied where the standard rent and the rateable valuation exceeded £20 and the landlord came into possession of the whole of the dwellinghouse at or after the passing of the Act. After coming into possession, the landlord let one room in the dwellinghouse to a tenant. The landlord sued to eject the tenant who claimed the protection of the Rent Acts. The Supreme Court, by a majority, rejected the tenant's claim that he was entitled to protection. Murnaghan J said:[3]

> the (1923) Act has ceased to apply to (the premises) under section 5 of the Act of 1926, and in my opinion it must also result that the (1923) Act has ceased to apply to fresh lettings of portions of these premises.

The effect of section 5(1) of the 1926 Act was reconsidered by the Supreme Court in *Logan v Donohue*.[4] Here the landlord had purchased a house in 1932 with vacant possession. In 1935 he let two rooms on the second floor of the house to two tenants. These rooms had formerly been let to one tenant and a standard rent had been fixed in 1924. The landlord contended that the Rent Acts had ceased to apply to the entire house by virtue of section 5(1). The Supreme Court held, however, that the two rooms remained subject to the provisions of the Acts. The court held that the two rooms in themselves constituted a dwellinghouse to which the 1923 Act applied and, because neither the standard rent nor the rateable valuation exceeded £20, the section 5(1) exclusion did not apply.

These decisions turn on the wording of the decontrolling section—section 5 (1) of the 1926 Act. This subsection decontrolled a 'dwellinghouse to which the (1923) Act applies' where the landlord recovered possession and the standard rent and the rateable valuation exceeded the prescribed limits. The subsection did not decontrol dwellinghouses in the ordinary sense of distinct structural units. In *Donnelly v O'Neill* the entire house had once been subject to a letting to which the 1923 Act applied. The landlord had gained possession

2. [1935] IR 286; 69 ILTR 205. See also *Gore-Grimes v Foley* 64 ILTR 52.
3. [1935] IR 286, 304.
4. [1938] IR 427; 73 ILTR 12.

and the standard rent and the rateable valuation exceeded the required limits; accordingly, the entire house was decontrolled by section 5(1). In *Logan v Donohue*, on the other hand, there was no evidence that the house as a whole was a dwellinghouse to which the Act applied. It was held that the two rooms let by the landlord after he came into possession were in themselves a statutory dwellinghouse (i.e., a dwellinghouse to which the 1923 Act applied) quite distinct from the dwellinghouse in its ordinary sense as one unit. And since the standard rent and rateable valuation of this statutory dwellinghouse did not exceed the required limit, it was held that this statutory dwellinghouse was not decontrolled by section 5(1), and so remained protected under the Acts.

Two conclusions can be drawn from these authorities. First, where a dwelling was decontrolled under the old legislation, then a subsequent letting of the dwelling, or a part of it, would not be recontrolled. This follows from the decision in *Donnelly v O'Neill*. Secondly, the decontrolling provision had to be carefully scrutinised to ascertain the precise entity which had been decontrolled. This is well illustrated by *Logan v Donohue* where, although the landlord had gained possession of the entire dwelling, a subsequent letting of part of the dwelling was held to be controlled. This was so because the decontrolling section relied upon by the landlord only applied to an artificial entity, namely, a 'dwellinghouse to which the (1923) Act applie(d)'; it did not apply to the house as a structural unit.

The application of the Landlord and Tenant Act to formerly controlled properties Both the 1960 and 1967 Act provided that the Landlord and Tenant Act 1931 would apply to certain properties decontrolled by their provisions. This gave the tenant the right in many cases to claim a new lease subject to his paying the market rent. The 1931 Act was repealed by Landlord and Tenant (Amendment) Act 1980. This Act also repealed the provisions of the 1960 and 1967 Rent Acts which applied the 1931 Act to decontrolled properties and, instead, extended its own provisions as to new tenancies to properties decontrolled by the Rent Acts. The application of the Landlord and Tenant Act to properties decontrolled by the 1960 and 1967 Acts is a matter of some complexity. Four separate statutory provisions have to be examined: section 54 of the 1960 Act, section 13 of the 1967 Act and sections 14 and 15 of the Landlord and Tenant (Amendment) Act 1980.

The application of the Landlord and Tenant Act to business premises decontrolled by the 1960 Act Section 54 of the 1960 Act applied the Landlord and Tenant Act 1931 to business premises which immediately before the commencement of the Act were controlled premises within the meaning of the Rent Restrictions Act 1946 provided the letting of the premises was neither made for temporary convenience nor dependent on the continuance of the tenant in any office, employment or appointment. If the premises were held under a statutory tenancy, the tenant was deemed to hold under a tenancy having the same terms and conditions as the statutory tenancy save that the landlord could determine the tenancy by not less than three months' notice.[5] Such a notice would be deemed a notice to quit.[6] It would be incumbent on a tenant who received such a notice to serve a notice of intention to claim relief within the prescribed time and then apply to the court to determine his right to relief in accordance with the provisions of the 1931 Act.

The application of the Landlord and Tenant Act to certain dwellings decontrolled by the 1967 Act Section 13 of the 1967 Act was similar in its effect to section 54. It applied the Landlord and Tenant Act 1931 to certain dwellings decontrolled by the 1967 Act. However, unlike section 54, section 13 expressly provided that the application of the Landlord and Tenant Act ceased on the landlord's coming into possession of the dwelling.[7] For section 13 to apply the dwelling had to be either a house or a separate and self-contained flat which immediately prior to 9 May 1967 was controlled and was neither subject to a letting made for temporary convenience nor a letting dependent on the continuance of the tenant in any office, employment or appointment.[8] The rateable valuation of the dwelling, if a house situate in Dublin or Dun Laoghaire, had to exceed £40; and, if situate elsewhere, had to exceed £30.[9] In the case of a separate and self-contained flat situate in Dublin or Dun Laoghaire the rateable valuation had to exceed £30; if situate elsewhere, the rateable valuation had to exceed £20.[10] Section 13 also applied the Landlord and Tenant Act 1931 to a house, the rateable valuation of which exceeded £10, where a bachelor or spinster over the age of 21 and under the age of 65 had become the tenant after 9 May 1967.[11]

If a house or flat affected by section 13 was held under a statutory tenancy, the tenant was deemed to hold under a tenancy having the same terms and conditions as the statutory tenancy save that the landlord could determine the tenancy by not less than three months' notice.[12] Such a notice would be

5. Rent Restrictions Act 1960, section 54(2)(v).
6. Ibid., section 54(2)(vi).
7. Rent Restrictions (Amendment) Act 1967, section 13(4).
8. Ibid., section 13(1).
9. Ibid.
10. Ibid.
11. Ibid., section 13(2).
12. Ibid., section 13(3)(iv) and (v).

deemed a notice to quit.[13] A tenant served with such a notice could then serve a notice of intention to claim relief and apply to the court for relief under the 1931 Landlord and Tenant Act.

Sections 14 and 15 of the Landlord and Tenant (Amendment) Act 1980 The 1980 Act repealed both section 54 of the 1960 Act and section 13 of the 1967 Act.[14] Section 54 is replaced by section 14 of the 1980 Act; section 13 is replaced by section 15 of the 1980 Act. Section 14 applies part II of the 1980 Act (relating to the tenant's right to a new tenancy) to business premises decontrolled by the 1960 Act provided the letting was not made for temporary convenience nor dependent on the continuance of the tenant in any office, employment or appointment.[15] Tenants of such decontrolled premises who held under a statutory tenancy prior to the commencement of the 1960 Act are deemed to hold under a tenancy having the same terms and conditions as the statutory tenancy terminable by three months' notice to quit.[16] It would appear that section 14 can only apply to premises which are wholly used for business purposes. If a dwelling is only partly used for business purposes, then it remains controlled and section 14 cannot be availed of.[17]

Section 15 applies part II of the 1980 Act to the dwellings formerly covered by section 13 of the 1967 Act.[18] Tenants of dwellings affected by section 15 who held under a statutory tenancy are also deemed to hold under a tenancy having the same terms and conditions as the statutory tenancy subject to termination by three months' notice to quit.[19] The right to claim a new tenancy by virtue of section 15 is, however, excluded on the landlord's coming into possession of the dwelling.[20]

The application of part II of the Landlord and Tenant (Amendment) Act 1980 Part II of the 1980 Act allows a tenant to claim a new tenancy. A tenant entitled to a new tenancy may either agree the terms with his landlord or apply to have the terms fixed by the court.[21] The court granting a new tenancy must fix a term of thirty-five years or such less term as the tenant may nominate.[22] The rent is to be the gross rent, reduced where appropriate by

13. Ibid., section 13(3)(vi).
14. Landlord and Tenant (Amendment) Act 1980, section 11(1) and the schedule.
15. Ibid., section 14(1).
16. Ibid., section 14(2).
17. See *Mullane v Brosnan* [1974] IR 222 and Rent Restrictions Act 1960, section 4.
18. Landlord and Tenant (Amendment) Act 1980, section 15(1) and (2).
19. Ibid., section 15(3) and (4).
20. Ibid., section 15(5).
21. Ibid., section 16.
22. Ibid., section 23(2).

any allowance made for improvements.[23] The gross rent is the rent which in the opinion of the court a willing lessee not already in occupation would give and a willing lessor would take on the basis of vacant possession being given.[24] The court is to have regard to the other terms of the tenancy and to the letting values of tenements of a similar character and situate in a comparable area, but is to disregard any goodwill which may exist in respect of the tenement.[25] An allowance may be made for improvements made by the tenant or his predecessors in title.[26] A tenant seeking a new tenancy must serve a notice of intention to claim relief in the prescribed form within the time limit specified in the Act.[27] But he is not entitled to a new tenancy where he has terminated the tenancy by notice of surrender or otherwise, or if the tenancy has been terminated on account of certain acts of default on his part.[28] Nor will the tenant be entitled where the landlord requires the premises for certain purposes, but a tenant in such a case is entitled to compensation for disturbance under part IV of the 1980 Act.[29] Where the terms of a new tenancy are fixed by the court, either party may apply to the court for a review of the rent after five years and thereafter after five years from the first or any subsequent review.[30]

Special provisions applicable where the dwelling is one to which section 15 relates If the terms of a new tenancy for a dwelling to which section 15 relates have not previously been fixed by the court under the 1931 Act or the 1980 Act and the court is satisfied that the rent which would otherwise be payable would cause hardship to the tenant, it must fix the rent under the new tenancy at a sum (not below the existing rent) which it is satisfied, having regard to all the circumstances of the case including any hardship to the landlord, the tenant should be required to pay.[31] The duration of the term fixed by the court may not, however, exceed ten years.[32]

23. Ibid., section 23(4).
24. Ibid., section 23(5).
25. Ibid.
26. Ibid., section 23(4) and (6).
27. Ibid., section 20 and see also section 83 for the circumstances in which the court can extend the time.
28. Ibid., section 17(1).
29. Ibid., section 17(2).
30. Landlord and Tenant (Amendment) Act 1984, section 15.
31. Landlord and Tenant (Amendment) Act 1980, section 25.
32. Ibid.

FOUR

The entitlement to retain possession

The right of the original tenant and the spouse A person who immediately before the commencement of the 1982 Act[1] was a tenant[2] of a dwelling controlled under the old legislation, other than one held under a tenancy for greater than from year to year or subject to a temporary convenience or service letting, is entitled to retain possession as tenant of the dwelling.[3] This tenant is referred to in the 1982 Act as the 'original tenant'. The entitlement to retain possession subsists for the original tenant's lifetime.[4] The spouse of the original tenant is entitled on the latter's death to retain possession as tenant of the dwelling if the spouse was bona fide residing in the dwelling at the time of death.[5] The entitlement subsists during the spouse's lifetime.[6]

The right of a member of the family of the original tenant A member of the original tenant's family[7] is entitled to retain possession as tenant of the dwelling where the original tenant, or a spouse who has become the tenant, dies within the relevant period, provided the member is bona fide residing in the dwelling at the date of death.[8] The relevant period is the period of twenty years beginning on the commencement of the 1982 Act.[9] The family

1. 26 July 1982: Housing (Private Rented Dwellings) Act 1982 (Commencement) Order 1982, SI No. 216 of 1982.
2. The term 'tenant' is defined in section 7(1) of the 1982 Act.
3. Housing (Private Rented Dwellings) Act 1982, section 9(1).
4. Ibid.
5. Ibid., section 9(2). The succession of the spouse is not regarded as an interest acquired under a settlement for the purpose of enactments relating to settled land: Housing (Private Rented Dwellings) Act 1982, section 22.
6. Ibid.
7. Under section 7(2) of the 1982 Act each of the following is deemed to be a member of the tenant's family: a father, mother, grandfather, grandmother, step-father, step-mother, father-in-law, mother-in-law, son, daughter, son-in-law, daughter-in-law, nephew, niece, grandson, granddaughter, step-son, step-daughter, brother, sister, half-brother, half-sister, uncle or aunt; or a person adopted by the tenant under the Adoption Acts 1952 to 1976, or the illegitimate offspring of the tenant, or a person to whom the tenant was *in loco parentis* and who was in bona fide residence with the tenant for not less than six years before his death.
8. Housing (Private Rented Dwellings) Act 1982, section 9(3).
9. Ibid., section 9(7).

member's entitlement commences on the date of death of the original tenant or spouse, and ends on the expiration of the relevant period.[10] If the family member who becomes the tenant dies within the relevant period, another member of the original tenant's family, if bona fide residing in the dwelling at the date of death, is entitled to retain possession as tenant of the dwelling.[11] Again the entitlement subsists from the date of death to the expiration of the relevant period.[12] Where there is more than one member of the original tenant's family bona fide residing in the dwelling at the time of the relevant death, the agreed member is to be the person entitled to retain possession.[13] In default of agreement, the member selected by the court is to be the person entitled.[14] If a family member becomes the tenant under the provisions of the Act, and there is less than five years of the relevant period remaining unexpired, the entitlement of the member subsists for a period of five years.[15]

Who is an original tenant? Section 9(1) of the 1982 Act curtly confers the right to retain possession on the original tenant, that is to say, the person who, immediately before the commencement of the Act, was the tenant of a controlled dwelling other than one held under a contract of tenancy for greater than from year to year or subject to a temporary convenience or service letting. The term 'tenant' is defined in section 7(1) of the 1982 Act as 'the person for the time being entitled to the possession of a dwelling to which section 8(1) relates and includes a person—(a) who would, at the commencement of this Act, be the tenant of the dwelling if the Rent Restrictions Act, 1960, and the Rent Restrictions (Amendment) Act 1967, had full force and effect at all times from their passing until such commencement, and (b) who is in possession of the dwelling at such commencement, and (c) whose tenancy is not a tenancy in respect of which an order for possession has been made under section 5 of the Rent Restrictions (Temporary Provisions) Act 1981.' This definition of 'tenant' in the 1982 Act contains two elements: firstly, a person for the time being entitled to possession of a controlled dwelling; and, secondly, a person who would be the tenant of the dwelling if the old legislation had full force and effect provided he is in possession and no order for possession has been made under section 5 of the 1981 Act.

The first element in the definition of the term 'tenant' is, on analysis, not particularly enlightening when determining whether a person is the original

10. Ibid., section 9(3).
11. Ibid., section 9(4).
12. Ibid.
13. Ibid., section 9(5).
14. Ibid.
15. Ibid., section 9(6).

tenant. It will be remembered that section 9(1) of the 1982 Act provides that an original tenant, being the tenant of a controlled dwelling, is entitled to retain possession. Turning to the definition of 'tenant', we find that he is the person for the time being entitled to possession. Put another way: the Act says that a person is entitled to retain possession of a controlled dwelling if he is the tenant; and also says that the tenant is the person entitled to possession.

Let us now consider the second element of the definition of 'tenant'—the person who would be the tenant of the dwelling if the Rent Restrictions Act 1960 and the Rent Restrictions (Amendment) Act 1967 had full force and effect at the commencement of the 1982 Act, provided he is in possession and no order for possession has been made under section 5 of the 1981 Act. Once again the old legislation, though buried, rules us from its grave. The critical point is to determine whether a person is a tenant under the old legislation. To do so, one must look to section 2(1) of the 1960 Act which provides that a tenant 'includes . . . a statutory tenant, and includes any person from time to time deriving title under the original tenant, and also includes a subtenant.' The term 'statutory tenant' is also defined in section 2(1). It includes the following persons who retain possession of a controlled dwelling: (1) a tenant, other than a tenant holding the dwelling under a temporary convenience or service letting, who retains possession of a controlled dwelling after his contractual tenancy has terminated:[16] (2) on termination of the tenant's interest, a subtenant to whom the dwelling or any part of it has been lawfully sublet;[17] (3) in certain cases the spouse or a member of a non-statutory tenant's family bona fide residing with him at the time of his death;[18] (4) the spouse or a member of a statutory tenant's family bona fide residing with him at the time of his death;[19] (5) the assignee of a statutory tenant where the dwelling is not used for the purposes of any business, trade or profession and, in certain circumstances, where it is so used;[20] and (6) a person who retains possession being a statutory tenant within the meaning of the Rent Restrictions Act 1946.[21] The position of some of these statutory tenants requires further examination.

The contractual tenant who retains possession after termination of his tenancy A tenant of a controlled dwelling who held over after the termination of his contractual tenancy retained possession under a statutory

16. Rent Restrictions Act 1960, section 2(1) and section 37.
17. Ibid., section 2(1) and section 31(2).
18. Ibid., section 2(1) and section 31(3).
19. Ibid., section 2(1) and section 31(4).
20. Ibid., section 2(1) and section 32 (5)(a)(iii) and (b).
21. Ibid., section 2(1) and section 52.

tenancy. So, for example, in *McCombe v Sheehan*,[22] where the tenant of a controlled dwelling held over after the expiration of the term of her lease and continued to pay rent which was accepted by the landlord, it was held that the implication of a yearly tenancy under section 5 of Deasy's Act[23] ought to give way to the inference that the tenant held as a statutory tenant under the Rent Acts. The termination of the contractual tenancy always had to be to be in accordance with the common law rules.[24]

The subtenant If the interest of the tenant of a controlled dwelling terminated, a subtenant was, under the 1960 Act, entitled to retain possession and to hold from the landlord as he would have held from the tenant.[25] An order for possession against a tenant did not affect the right to retain possession of any subtenant to whom the dwelling or any part of it had been lawfully sublet prior to the commencement of the proceedings.[26] Thus in *Sisk v Cronin*[27] the tenant of a controlled dwelling went to live elsewhere and his brother went into residence of the dwelling with his permission. The Supreme Court held that the proper inference from the evidence was that the brother occupied the dwelling as the tenant's tenant at will and was entitled to retain possession, notwithstanding that possession was ordered against the tenant, as the dwelling had been lawfully sublet to him prior to the commencement of the proceedings. The onus of proving that the subtenancy was not lawful rested on the landlord.[28] Service by him of a notice to quit, it was held in two cases, constituted the commencement of proceedings, so that a subletting made thereafter was not protected.[29] The Supreme Court, however, disapproved of these decisions in *Waldron v Burbage*.[30]

A point on which there is conflicting authority was whether a subtenancy could be controlled where the original letting was not controlled. In *O'Brien v Wallace*[31] the landlord let two rooms to a trade union as a meeting place for its members. The union sublet one room to a shoemaker for the purposes of his trade. The landlord brought ejectment proceedings and recovered

22. [1954] IR 183; 88 ILTR 114.
23. Landlord and Tenant Amendment Act (Ireland) 1860.
24. For detailed exposition of the termination of tenancies see Deale, *The Law of Landlord and Tenant in the Republic of Ireland* (Dublin, 1968), chapter 6 and Wylie, *Irish Landlord and Tenant Law* (Dublin, 1990), chapters 23 and 24.
25. Rent Restrictions Act 1960, section 31(2).
26. Ibid., section 30.
27. [1930] IR 98. See also *Waldron v Burbage* 91 ILTR 30 where a statutory tenant sublet the entire premises of which he was tenant it was held that the subtenant was entitled to the protection of the Rent Acts.
28. *Lewis v Shepperson* [1947] Ir Jur Rep 47.
29. *Constantine v Darcy* 68 ILTR 27; *Martin v Mulligan* [1943] Ir Jur Rep 43.
30. 91 ILTR 30.
31. [1932] IR 308.

possession from the union. He then brought proceedings against the subtenant who claimed the protection of the 1923 Rent Act. The High Court rejected the argument that, because the letting was outside the Act, the subletting was also outside the Act; and held that the subtenant was protected. But in *Marsham v CIE*[32] it was held that, where the tenant under a lease was not entitled to the protection of the 1946 Rent Act, the tenant's subtenants, though within the limits for protection, were not entitled to the protection of the Act. Both *O'Brien v Wallace* and *Marsham v CIE* were considered in *O'Farrell v Woods*[33] where Judge Deale, whose decision was affirmed on appeal to the High Court, expressed the view that *O'Brien v Wallace* was still good law. Referring to the decision in *O'Brien*, he said:[34] 'From this case it appears to me to follow that it is legally possible to create, out of an uncontrolled premises, a subletting of a premises which will thereby become a controlled premises.'

Where a tenant sublet a controlled dwelling, otherwise than for temporary convenience, the 1960 Act provided that the statutory restrictions on the landlord's right to recover possession against the tenant did not apply; but the subtenant or any person deriving title under him would be protected.[35] The protection against ejectment for the subtenant was no greater than that afforded to a tenant.[36] So, if the landlord could establish the existence of one of the statutory grounds entitling him to possession, and showed that it was reasonable to make an order against the subtenant, the court might order the eviction of the subtenant.

The spouse and members of the tenant's family Section 31 of the 1960 Act provided for the transmission of the entitlement to possession on the death of a contractual or statutory tenant to his spouse or other member of his family bona fide residing with him at the time of death. The provisions of section 31 are complex. To understand them one must bear in mind that, apart from section 31, where a contractual tenant died his tenancy, like his other property, formed part of his estate and passed to his personal representative. The personal representative was then bound to dispose of the tenancy in accordance with the directions contained in the will or in accordance with the rules applicable to an intestacy as the case might be. However, a landlord could, of course, terminate the tenancy after the tenant died. If he

32. [1953] IR 33.
33. [1957] Ir Jur Rep 26.
34. [1957] Ir Jur Rep 26, 30.
35. Rent Restrictions Act 1960, section 29(3); see also section 47 of the 1960 Act empowering the landlord to attorn the part of a dwelling sublet by the tenant for business purposes or, where the tenant retained part of the dwelling for business purposes, the remainder sublet by him which became a controlled dwelling.
36. *Enniskillen UDC v Bartley* [1947] NI 177.

did so, section 31 of the 1960 Act intervened to provide for the transmission of the tenancy to the tenant's spouse or a member of his family. Thus section 31(3) of the 1960 Act provided that where a contractual tenant died intestate and the tenancy was terminated before administration was granted or during administration of the estate or, in any other case, where the tenancy terminated while the executor was not in occupation of the dwelling, then the surviving spouse bona fide residing with the tenant at the time of death was entitled to retain possession on the same terms and conditions as the deceased tenant. If the contractual tenant did not leave a spouse bona fide residing with him at the time of death, a member of his family so residing was entitled to retain possession.[37] If there was more than one member, the member agreed upon between them or selected by the court in default of agreement was entitled.[38]

Section 31(4) laid down the same scheme in relation to statutory tenancies. The surviving spouse bona fide residing with a statutory tenant at the time of his death was entitled to retain possession on the same terms and conditions. A member of the statutory tenant's family[39] bona fide residing with him at the time of death was entitled where no spouse was left.[40] If there was more than one member, the member agreed upon or selected by the court was entitled to retain possession.[41] The interest terminated if there was no spouse or member of the statutory tenant's family entitled to succeed to his interest.[42]

The assignee Section 32 of the 1960 Act provided that it was a condition of a statutory tenancy that a tenant could not assign the dwelling, or any part of it, without the landlord's written consent.[43] But the landlord's consent to an assignment could only be withheld if greater hardship would be caused by granting the consent than by withholding it.[44] Where a controlled dwelling was lawfully assigned by a statutory tenant on or after 31 December 1960 and was, at the date of the assignment, lawfully used in part for the purposes of any business, trade, or profession, then, in the absence of any express agreement between the landlord and the assignee, the assignee was deemed to hold the dwelling in accordance with the appropriate paragraph under section 32(5)(a) of the 1960 Act. If the dwelling was not used for the purposes of any business, trade or profession, and there was no express agreement

37. Rent Restrictions Act 1960, section 31(3).
38. Ibid.
39. 'Family' for the purposes of subsections (3) and (4) was defined in section 31(5).
40. Rent Restrictions Act 1960, section 31(4).
41. Ibid.
42. Ibid.
43. Ibid., section 32(4)(b).
44. Ibid.

between the landlord and the assignee, then the assignee was entitled to retain possession on the same terms and conditions as the assignor.[45]

Section 10 of the 1967 Act provided that the tenant of a controlled dwelling, other than a dwelling lawfully used in part for the purposes of any business, trade or profession, could not assign his tenancy without the written consent of the landlord unless the contract of tenancy was in writing and contained a provision authorising assignment without the landlord's consent.[46] The consent could be withheld only if the assignment was otherwise than to a member of the tenant's family who was bona fide residing with him at the time of the assignment.[47] An assignment in contravention of these provisions was void.[48]

It will be noted that the restriction on assignment in the 1960 Act applied only to statutory tenancies. The restriction in the 1967 Act applied, on the other hand, to controlled dwellings other than those used in part for business purposes; for the purpose of the 1967 Act restriction, it was immaterial whether the tenancy was statutory or contractual. There was, therefore, one class of controlled dwelling which was unaffected by the restrictions on assignment in either the 1960 or 1967 Acts—a controlled dwelling used in part for business purposes held under a contractual tenancy. In such a case the provisions of section 66 of the Landlord and Tenant (Amendment) Act 1980 might apply. This section effectively prevents a landlord from unreasonably withholding his consent to an assignment.[49]

The requirement that the tenant be in possession The 1982 Act protects the tenant who, as we have seen, is 'the person for the time being entitled to possession of a (controlled) dwelling'. The Act does not expressly require that the tenant be in actual occupation; but, historically, the rule has been that the tenant must be in occupation of the dwelling in order to claim the protection of the Rent Acts. This rule was authoritatively laid down by the Supreme Court in *Foley v Galvin*.[50] There Fitzgibbon J held[51] that:

45. Ibid., section 32(5)(b).
46. Rent Restrictions (Amendment) Act 1967, section 10(2)(a).
47. Rent Restrictions (Amendment) Act 1967, section 10(2)(b).
48. Ibid., section 10(3).
49. See Deale, *The Landlord and Tenant Acts 1931 and 1943* (Dublin, 1953), pp. 94-99, dealing with section 56 of the Landlord and Tenant Act 1931 which corresponds to section 66 of the 1980 Act; and see Wylie, *Irish Landlord and Tenant Law*, op. cit., paras 21.09-21.11.
50. [1932] IR 339; 66 ILTR 169; [1932] LJ Ir 113.
51. [1932] IR 339, 361-2.

> the tenant who is entitled to retain possession of his dwelling-house, and who is protected from ejectment therefrom, notwithstanding the determination of his tenancy by efflux of time or notice to quit, is a tenant who is in actual occupation by himself or some member of his family or a caretaker, or who, though not at the moment in actual occupation, does in fact require the dwelling-house for his own use.

Kennedy CJ held that the Acts were passed to benefit occupying tenants, but observed[52] that 'continuous personal residence is not . . . always necessary to constitute the possession of an occupying tenant.' So what amounts to an 'entitlement to possession' sufficient to attract protection under the 1982 Act is a question which has to be resolved by the courts; it is a question which not infrequently troubled them in the past.

The decision in *Foley v Galvin* was applied in *Caulfield v Kenny*[53] so as to preclude a tenant who did not reside in the premises and who had sublet a portion of them from applying to have the standard rent determined under the 1923 Act. In *Gore-Grimes v Flynn*[54] where the tenant of a controlled dwelling moved with most of his family into a local authority house, but left some members of the family in the controlled dwelling, it was held that he did not occupy the dwelling and, consequently, could not claim protection under the Acts. Likewise in *McArdle Moore & Co. Ltd v Kelly*,[55] it was held that the tenant was not protected where he did not reside in the dwelling, but planned to return to it in the event he lost his job. And in *McErlane v McGowan*[56] it was held that a person prohibited by law from residing in premises cannot be in possession through a servant or agent.

But the requirement of possession has not invariably been rigorously applied. Occupation by orphan nieces and dependent children was sufficient to qualify for protection in *Walsh v Byrne*.[57] Protection under the 1946 Act was granted in *Walsh v Coyne*[58] where the tenant came to the premises every morning and left about midnight; he had all his meals on the premises; he slept there about once a fortnight; and in evidence he stated his intention to move his wife and family into the premises. A garda inspector who was the statutory tenant of premises in Cork was held entitled to protection under the 1946 Act in *McCabe v McGonigle*;[59] he was transferred from Cork but left

52. [1932] IR 339, 353.
53. [1935] IR 272; 69 ILTR 190.
54. [1932] LJ Ir 165.
55. 94 ILTR 48.
56. 78 ILTR 106.
57. [1940] Ir Jur Rep 13.
58. [1958] IR 223; 92 ILTR 84.
59. [1956] IR 162.

his furniture in the premises and continued to pay the rent, and his sister continued to occupy the premises. Finally, the tenant was allowed the protection of the 1946 Act in *White v White*[60] although she did not reside in the premises, but visited them annually in order to see her parents and invalid sister who were in occupation.

Where the tenant resumed occupation after service of a notice to quit, it was held that she was not entitled to claim the protection of the Rent Act.[61] But the position may be otherwise where the court is satisfied that the resumption of possession is bona fide.[62]

Cessation of the entitlement to possession Entitlement to retain possession of a controlled dwelling ceases to subsist where possession of the dwelling is recovered by the landlord.[63] The term 'landlord' is defined in section 2(1) of the 1982 Act as 'the person for the time being entitled to receive (otherwise than as agent for another person) the rent payable in respect of a dwelling'. Protection afforded by the Act also ceases, as we have seen, where the tenant assigns or sublets his tenancy or where his entitlement to retain possession ceases to subsist.[64]

Surrender of a controlled dwelling The tenant of a controlled dwelling may surrender the dwelling to the landlord on giving him not less than one month's notice in writing of his intention to surrender.[65] The surrender of a controlled dwelling in this way operates as the conveyance of an interest for the purposes of the Family Home Protection Act 1976.[66]

60. 90 ILTR 52.
61. *Lynch v Fitzgerald* 80 ILTR 107.
62. *Hardwicke Ltd v Murphy* 85 ILTR 59.
63. Housing (Private Rented Dwellings) Act 1982, section 9(8).
64. Ibid., section 8(3).
65. Ibid., section 10(1).
66. Ibid., section 10(2).

FIVE

The terms of a tenancy of a controlled dwelling

The terms of a tenancy of a controlled dwelling may be agreed between the landlord and tenant or, in default of agreement, fixed by the Rent Tribunal.[1] If the Minister for the Environment makes the necessary order under section 6(1) of the 1983 Act, the terms will be fixed by a rent officer from whose determination an appeal will lie to the tribunal.[2] The jurisdiction to fix the terms of a tenancy was formerly exercised by the District Court under section 12 of the 1982 Act, but it is no longer possible to apply to the court to fix the terms.[3]

The power of the tribunal or rent officer to fix the terms Section 5 of the 1983 Act deals with applications to the tribunal or rent officer to fix the terms of a tenancy of a controlled dwelling. The landlord or tenant may apply at any time for an order fixing the terms.[4] The applicant must give one month's notice in writing to the other party of his intention to make the application.[5] The terms of the tenancy, once determined by the tribunal or rent officer, are binding on both parties unless new terms are fixed under the 1983 Act.[6] An application to fix the terms of a tenancy may be made notwithstanding any agreement between the landlord and tenant fixing the terms, and it does not matter that the agreement was made before or after the commencement of section 5.[7] If any dispute or question arises in the interpretation of a determination, an application may be made by either party to the tribunal or rent officer to resolve the matter.[8] Where the terms are fixed under the 1983 Act or have been fixed by the District Court under the 1982 Act, no further

1. Housing (Private Rented Dwellings) (Amendment) Act 1983, section 7(1).
2. Ibid., section 11(1).
3. Ibid., section 5(6).
4. Ibid., section 5(1).
5. Ibid., section 5(5) and see the Housing (Rent Tribunal) Regulations 1983, SI No. 222 of 1983 as to procedural matters.
6. Housing (Private Rented Dwellings) (Amendment) Act 1983, section 5(1).
7. Ibid., section 5(2).
8. Ibid., section 5(4).

application may be made to fix the terms until the expiration of four years and nine months from the date on which the terms were last fixed.[9] But if the landlord has carried out improvements to the dwelling, the application may be made before the expiration of this period.[10] An 'improvement' is defined as 'any addition to or alteration of a dwelling which adds to the letting value of the dwelling and includes any addition or alteration connected with the provision of any services to the dwelling, but does not include work of repairing, decorating or normal maintenance'.[11]

Fixing of the rent by the tribunal or rent officer Where the terms of a tenancy are fixed by the tribunal or rent officer, the rent of the dwelling is to be the gross rent reduced by any allowance for improvements.[12] The gross rent is to be the rent which, in the opinion of the tribunal or rent officer, would be a just and proper rent having regard to the matters set out in section 13(2) of the 1982 Act, that is to say, the nature, character and location of the dwelling, the other terms of the tenancy, the means of the landlord and the tenant,[13] the date of purchase of the dwelling by the landlord and the amount paid by him for it, the length of the tenant's occupancy of the dwelling and the number and ages of the tenant's family residing in the dwelling.[14] The application of these various criteria by the tribunal was considered by the Supreme Court in *Quirke v Folio Homes Ltd.*[15] McCarthy J expressed the view[16] that the criteria could be divided into three categories. The first of these—the nature, character and location of the dwelling—he termed the 'objective' criteria. The means of the landlord and the tenant fell into a second category which he described as 'personal but potentially common to both sides'. The third category, 'matters capable of exact detail and touching upon the second category', consisted of the date of purchase by the landlord and the amount paid by him, the length of the tenant's occupancy and the number and ages of his family. These criteria, McCarthy J concluded,[17] 'are not in the nature of an automatic check list; they are only to be considered when

9. Ibid., section 5(3)(a).
10. Ibid.
11. Ibid., section 5(3)(b).
12. Housing (Private Rented Dwellings) Act 1982, section 13(1) and Housing (Private Rented Dwellings) (Amendment) Act 1983, section 9(2).
13. The means of the tenant refer to his actual means: Housing (Private Rented Dwellings) (Amendment) Act 1983, section 9(3).
14. Housing (Private Rented Dwellings) Act 1982, section 13(2) and Housing (Private Rented Dwellings) (Amendment) Act 1983, section 9(2). See *Jephson v Mortell* [1949] Ir Jur Rep 3 and *Boland v Hewson* [1950] Ir Jur Rep 13.
15. [1988] ILRM 496.
16. At p. 499 of the report.
17. At p. 500 of the report.

they are relevant; all those in category 1 must always be relevant but those in category 2 and 3 are only made relevant in certain circumstances'.

The particular issue in the *Quirke* case was the extent to which the tribunal should take into account the landlord's means in fixing the rent. The landlord was a company, Folio Homes Ltd, which in April 1979 had purchased 651 houses (including that occupied by Mr Quirke) for just over £808,000. At the hearing before the tribunal, when asked about the company's means, its solicitor told the tribunal that its income was greater than that of the tenant. The tribunal proceeded to deal with the matter on that basis and the rent, which had been 88 pence per week, was fixed at £16 per week. On appeal to the High Court the tenant claimed that the tribunal had erred in failing to make adequate enquiries into the landlord's means and in failing to have adequate regard to those means. The approach taken by the tribunal was upheld by the Supreme Court. 'It is manifest,' said McCarthy J,[18] 'that the ruling of the Tribunal was founded upon a construction of section 13(2) which made the means of the landlord a relevant consideration only when the landlord sought to make it so; when the landlord sought, as it were, to offset a plea of financial hardship made on the part of the tenant or in some other fashion sought to argue that the rent should be adjusted upwards because of such potential hardship to the landlord. In my judgment, this construction was correct and the consequent ruling equally so.'

A conspicuous omission from the matters in section 13(2), to which the tribunal or rent officer may have regard, are the rents charged for other similar controlled dwellings. This contrasts markedly with the position of the Circuit Court when fixing the rent on an application for a new tenancy under part II of the Landlord and Tenant (Amendment) Act 1980; the Circuit Court is empowered by section 23(5) of that Act to have regard to 'the letting values of tenements of a similar character to the tenement and situate in a comparable area'. The omission of a comparability criterion may be taken as an indicator that the rent fixed by the tribunal is not to be a 'market' rent in the sense that it is related to rents payable for other dwellings. The emphasis in section 13(2) is on a 'just and proper rent'. Again this contrasts with the position under the Landlord and Tenant Act where the gross rent is defined as 'the rent which in the opinion of the Court a willing lessee not already in occupation would give and a willing lessor would take'.

Included in section 13(2) among the things which the tribunal may take into account are 'the other terms of the tenancy'. These terms may include the liability to insure the dwelling, the liability for repairs, and so forth. A problem which not infrequently arises in practice is the approach to be taken when a covenant has not been complied with, as, for example, happened in

18. At p. 499 of the report.

the case of *Dowd v Pierce*.[19] This case (which pre-dated the 1983 Act) concerned an application to the District Court to fix the rent. The evidence disclosed that the premises were in a poor overall state of repair; the landlord had failed to comply with his covenant to repair the exterior and, in consequence, the interior, for which the tenant was responsible, was also in need of repair. The District Court fixed the rent on the hypothetical basis that both parties had complied with their respective obligations to repair. On appeal to the Circuit Court, however, it was held that the hypothetical approach was wrong and the court adjourned the application to enable the landlord to perform the necessary external repairs.

The allowance for improvements As we have seen, the tribunal or rent officer when fixing the rent may make an allowance for improvements.[20] That allowance is to be such proportion of the gross rent as is, in the opinion of the tribunal or rent officer, attributable to improvements.[21] An 'improvement' is defined for this purpose in section 7(1) of the 1982 Act as 'any addition to or alteration of a dwelling carried out by a tenant or any of his predecessors in title on or after 31 December 1960, which adds to the letting value of the dwelling and includes any addition or alteration connected with the provision of any services to the dwelling, but does not include work of repairing (except where such work was the responsibility of the landlord and he failed to carry out the work), painting and decorating or any of them.' The erection of a shed in the yard at the back of a small house was found, in *Ryan v Phelan*,[22] to be an improvement. But the Supreme Court, in *Rabbitt v Grant*,[23] held that the installation of a water closet was a repair and not an improvement for the purposes of the 1923 Rent Act.

Payment of an increased rent If the rent of a controlled dwelling is increased, whether by agreement between the parties or on foot of an application to the Rent Tribunal or a rent officer, the amount of the increase is not payable until a written statement of the terms of the tenancy signed by the landlord or his agent has been made out and a copy furnished to the tenant, and the requirements laid down in the Housing (Private Rented Dwellings) Regulations 1982[24] as to registration of the tenancy and the furnishing to the

19. [1984] ILRM 653.
20. Housing (Private Rented Dwellings) Act 1982, section 13(1) and Housing (Private Rented Dwellings) (Amendment) Act 1983, section 9(2).
21. Ibid.
22. [1940] Ir Jur Rep 56.
23. [1940] IR 323; 74 ILTR 76.
24. SI No. 217 of 1982 as amended by the Housing (Private Rented Dwellings) (Amendment) Regulations 1983, SI No. 286 of 1983.

housing authority of particulars of the new rent have been complied with.[25] Where the rent is fixed by the tribunal or a rent officer, it is payable from the first gale day after the tenant has been furnished with the written statement of the terms of the tenancy and the registration requirements have been complied with.[26] On a subsequent application the new rent applies from whichever of the following dates is the later: the first gale day after the terms have been furnished to the tenant and the registration requirements complied with or the date which is five years after the date from which the old rent first applied.[27] But where an early application is made on account of the landlord having carried out improvements, the new rent is payable on the first gale day after the furnishing of the terms and registration.[28]

The other terms of the tenancy Apart from fixing the rent, the Rent Tribunal, as has been noted, may have to determine the other terms of the tenancy. In doing so the tribunal may have regard for the existing terms; but in many cases the parties, for whatever reason, cannot assist the tribunal on the terms of the tenancy and there is no clear evidence as to what they are. In practice the tribunal tends to make the tenant subject to the following obligations: he has to pay any rates assessed on the dwelling; he has to permit the landlord to enter the dwelling during reasonable hours for the purpose of carrying out any works for which the landlord is liable; he must not make any structural alterations without the landlord's express written consent; he must keep the interior of the dwelling in good and tenantable order, repair and condition; he must keep the garden in good order; he must not cause a nuisance or annoyance to the landlord or adjoining occupiers; and he must use the dwelling as a private residence only. The landlord, on the other hand, may be required to keep the structure and exterior of the dwelling, and every part of it for which the tenant is not liable, in good, repair and condition. He may also be bound to keep the dwelling insured against loss or damage by fire in its full reinstatement value; and in case of destruction or damage, to lay out the money received in respect of the insurance in rebuilding or reinstating the dwelling; and if that money is insufficient for the purpose, to make good the deficiency out of his own money.

The liability for repairs The question of the liability for repairs is an important one in the context of controlled dwellings if only because so many of them are in a poor state of repair.[29] In practice, when fixing the terms, the

25. Housing (Private Rented Dwellings) (Amendment) Act 1983, section 7(2).
26. Ibid., section 8(1).
27. Ibid., section 8(2)(a).
28. Ibid., section 8(2)(b).
29. See the comments in the Rent Tribunal, Annual Report and Accounts 1983/84, p. 8, in relation to the standards of dwellings and see below, pp. 48-9, in relation to the Housing

Rent Tribunal frequently divides the responsibility making the tenant liable for the interior and the landlord liable for the exterior. But this is not invariably the case and the tribunal may have regard to the existing arrangement, particularly where there is a written tenancy agreement indicating on whom the liability for repairs falls. But if the agreement is silent on the point, or if there is no written agreement and the parties have made no arrangement about repairs, it may then be difficult to know who is responsible.

Under section 42 of the Landlord and Tenant Law Amendment Act, Ireland, 1860 (Deasy's Act) it is an implied term of every lease that the tenant is to 'keep the premises in good and substantial repair and condition, unless otherwise expressly provided'. But if express provision is made in the lease, that provision is an exhaustive statement of the tenant's liability. So, in *Cowan v Factor*[30] where the lease made the tenant liable for repair of the interior of the premises, it was held that section 42 did not imply any further agreement as to repairs and, accordingly, that the tenant was not liable for external repairs. The court in *Cowan's* case refused to follow the decision in *Kiernan v O'Connell*[31] where it was held that the tenant was liable for external repairs under section 42 of Deasy's Act, even though the letting agreement only obliged him to repair the interior. Later, in *Gray v Siev*,[32] Judge O Briain attempted to reconcile the two decisions, but expressed the view that the decision in *Cowan's* case was 'more consistent with the settled general principle'.

It must be borne in mind that section 42 of Deasy's Act only applies to a lease which is defined in section 1 as an 'instrument in writing'. If the tenancy is an oral one and there is no agreement in relation to repair, then it seems that there is no duty on either party, save of course that the tenant would be liable should he commit acts of waste. In a very old case, *Auworth v Johnson*,[33] it was held that a tenant under an oral agreement was not bound to repair; but was bound to keep the dwelling wind and watertight. On the other hand, in *Scales v Vandeleur*,[34] a landlord of two adjoining premises, who had not been in possession of them other than through a tenant for fifty years, was held not to be liable to the tenant for the dangerous condition of the premises in the absence of an express covenant to repair.[35] But a landlord

(Private Rented Dwellings) (Standards) Regulations 1984 which came into force on 1 April 1985 and apply to dwellings controlled under the 1982 Act.

30. [1948] IR 128; 83 ILTR 99.
31. 72 ILTR 196.
32. 83 ILTR 67, 68.
33. 5 C & P 239.
34. 48 ILTR 36.
35. Here, of course, we are discussing the position of a private landlord; it is well established that a housing authority is bound by an implied warranty that premises let by it are fit for human habitation: *Siney v Dublin Corporation* [1980] IR 400 and *Coleman v Dundalk UDC* unreported decision of the Supreme Court, judgment delivered 17 July 1985.

may be liable in negligence to his tenant for loss sustained by him arising out of the landlord's failure to take reasonable care to prevent any part of the premises over which he (the landlord) has retained control from becoming a source of danger or damage.[36]

If in the past a contractual tenancy, be it created by lease or oral agreement, terminated, with the result that the tenancy became a statutory one under the Rent Restrictions Acts, section 32(4)(c) of the 1960 Act made the landlord responsible for any repairs for which the tenant was not liable. This provision was supplemented by section 11 of the 1967 Act which provided that, where the landlord of a controlled dwelling subject to a weekly or monthly letting had obtained a lawful addition to the basic rent on account of his liability for repairs, certain covenants as to repairs were to be implied on his part. Specifically, he was bound to keep in repair the structure of the dwelling; the exterior (including drains, gutters and external pipes, window frames and exterior doors); the installations in the dwelling for the supply of water and gas and for sanitation; and in the case of a flat, he was bound to keep the ceiling in repair.

Finally, it may be noted that under the Housing Act 1966, section 114(1) it is provided that there is an implied undertaking by the landlord in any contract for the letting of a house for habitation at a rent not exceeding £130 per annum that the house will be kept reasonably fit for human habitation. This obligation had formerly been placed on the landlord by section 31(1) of the Housing (Miscellaneous Provisions) Act 1931 in respect of a house let at a rent not exceeding £30 in Dublin or Dun Laoghaire, or £25 if situate elsewhere. The landlord's obligation under the Housing Act does not apply to the purchase of a house by way of a long lease.[37]

Compensation for improvements The tenant of a controlled dwelling is entitled under section 15 of the 1982 Act to be paid compensation for improvements on quitting the dwelling. The amount of the compensation is to be such sum as may be agreed between the landlord and the tenant or, in default of agreement, as is determined by the District Court.[38] A tenant seeking compensation for improvements under section 15 must serve a claim in writing on the landlord giving all particulars relevant to the claim.[39] The

36. *Byrne v Martina Investments Ltd*, unreported judgment of the High Court (O'Hanlon J) delivered 30 January 1984; *Victor Weston (Éire) Ltd v Kenny* [1954] IR 191.
37. *McGowan v Harrison* [1941] IR 331; 75 ILTR 163.
38. Housing (Private Rented Dwellings) Act 1982, section 15(1).
39. Ibid., section 15(4). See the District Court [Housing (Private Rented Dwellings) Act 1982] Rules 1982, SI No. 296 of 1982, as to the form of the notice of application and procedural matters.

claim may be served either before or after the tenant has quit the dwelling, but may not be served later than three months after quitting.[40] Where the court determines a claim for compensation the amount awarded is to be the capitalised value of the addition to the letting value of the dwelling at the time of quitting which is attributable to the improvements.[41] In determining the amount the court is to have regard to the probable life of the improvements and all other relevant circumstances.[42] The court may deduct such sum from the compensation as it considers reasonable in two cases: (1) if it is satisfied that benefits by way of reduction of rent or otherwise have been received by the tenant, or his predecessors in title, from the landlord in consideration of the improvements; or (2) to compensate the landlord for rent due or loss incurred arising from reasons for which an order for possession has been granted.[43] The compensation is to be paid in such manner and over such period as may be agreed or as the court may direct.[44]

A tenant is not entitled to compensation for improvements under section 15 where compensation has been paid in respect of the dwelling under part IV of the Landlord and Tenant (Amendment) Act 1980.[45] And where compensation is paid under section 15, no right to compensation lies under part IV of the 1980 Act.[46] Nor is a tenant entitled to compensation for improvements made in contravention of any obligation of the tenancy agreement under which the dwelling was let unless the court considers that, in the circumstances, the carrying out of the improvements was reasonable.[47]

40. Ibid.
41. Ibid., section 15(2).
42. Ibid.
43. Ibid., section 15(3).
44. Ibid., section 15(5).
45. Ibid., section 15(6)(b).
46. Ibid., section 15(7).
47. Ibid., section 15(6)(a).

SIX

Standards and registration of rented dwellings

Standards for rented dwellings The Minister for the Environment is empowered by section 26 of the 1982 Act to make regulations prescribing standards for any class of rented dwelling. These regulations may prescribe standards in relation to: (1) the quality and condition of the accommodation, furnishings and appliances; (2) the maintenance of dwellings in good repair and in an adequate state of cleanliness; (3) ventilation and lighting; (4) the provision of water supplies, sanitary facilities and drainage; (5) heating and cooking; and (6) accommodation for the storage of and facilities for the preparation of food.[1]

The Housing (Private Rented Dwellings) (Standards) Regulations 1984, SI No. 337 of 1984, came into force on 1 April 1985 and apply to dwellings controlled under the 1982 Act.[2] These dwellings must be maintained in a proper state of structural repair[3] and the landlord is bound to carry out such works as may from time to time be necessary for that purpose.[4] He must provide, either in the dwelling or in a part of the building adjacent to the dwelling, a sink, a fixed bath or shower and a watercloset for which there must be a piped supply of water together with an effective means of

1. Housing (Private Rented Dwellings) Act 1982, section 26(2).
2. Housing (Private Rented Dwellings) (Standards) Regulations 1984, articles 2 and 4: in the case of a dwelling for which the terms of the tenancy were set out in written form and signed by the landlord or his agent in accordance with section 11(2) of the 1982 Act before 1 April 1985, the regulations came into operation on 1 January 1988, or when the rent of the dwelling is fixed by the Rent Tribunal, whichever is earlier. The introduction of uniform minimum standards for other dwellings in the private rented sector is likely to take place in the future: see *A Plan for Social Housing* published by the Department of the Environment in February 1991.
3. The requirements in the regulations in relation to repair are to be construed as requiring a standard of repair which is reasonable in all the circumstances and, in determining the standard, regard is to be had to the age, character and prospective life of the dwelling: Housing (Private Rented Dwellings) (Standards) Regulations 1984, article 3(2).
4. Housing (Private Rented Dwellings) (Standards) Regulations 1984, article 5(1).

drainage.[5] Installations in the dwelling for the supply of gas and electricity must be in good repair and safe working order and provision must be made for the safe removal of fumes to the external air.[6] The landlord must ensure that every habitable room is provided with adequate lighting and ventilation and that all windows and other means of ventilation are in good order and repair, but he is not bound to make good breakages of glass in windows in any part of the dwelling of which the tenant has exclusive use.[7] Bedrooms, bathrooms and waterclosets must be properly ventilated and there must be adequate means for the artificial lighting of every room.[8] Finally, the landlord has certain obligations where certain services and areas are used in common. He must (*inter alia*) keep in a clean state and in good repair every open space, stairway, landing, passage and other part of the building which is used by the tenant in common with others and ensure that boundary walls, fences and railings are kept in reasonable repair so as not to constitute a danger to the occupants of the dwelling.[9]

Enforcement of these regulations is the responsibility of the housing authority whose inspectors are empowered to enter and inspect dwellings to which the regulations apply.[10] Moreover, where a regulation is not being complied with, a housing authority may, after giving not less than 21 days' notice in writing to the landlord and the tenant, carry out any work necessary to ensure that the dwelling complies with the regulations.[11] It may recover the expenses reasonably incurred in the work from the landlord as a simple contract debt.[12] A landlord upon whom a notice has been served may appeal to the District Court to have it set aside and, pending the determination of the appeal, the housing authority may not carry out any work.[13]

Registration A system for the registration of rented accommodation is provided for in the 1982 Act by section 24. The Minister for the Environment is empowered to make regulations requiring the landlords of any class of rented dwelling to register the tenancy of each dwelling with the housing

5. Ibid., article 6(1), (2) and (4).
6. Ibid., article 7.
7. Ibid., article 8.
8. Ibid.
9. Ibid., article 9.
10. Housing (Private Rented Dwellings) Act 1982, section 27(3) and section 26(3). Obstruction of an inspector is an offence: Housing (Private Rented Dwellings) Act 1982, section 27(1).
11. Ibid., section 26(4).
12. Ibid.
13. Ibid., section 26(5).

authority in whose functional area the dwelling is situated.[14] A landlord is obliged to furnish such particulars as the regulations require including his name and address, the name and address of the tenant and the amount of the rent.[15] An application to register a dwelling is to be accompanied by such fee as the minister may from time to time prescribe.[16] In addition, section 24 requires each housing authority to keep a register of all dwellings governed by the regulations in its functional area.[17] The register is to be kept at the offices of the housing authority and is to be available for inspection during normal office hours.[18]

Rent books Section 25 of the 1982 Act empowers the Minister for the Environment to make regulations requiring the landlords of any class of rented dwelling to provide rent books to their tenants. The regulations are to prescribe the particulars to be contained in the rent book, the requirements regarding its use and such other matters as the minister considers necessary.[19]

The Housing (Private Rented Dwellings) Regulations 1982 Regulations have been made implementing the provisions of sections 24 and 25: the Housing (Private Rented Dwellings) Regulations 1982 (SI No. 217 of 1982) which came into force on 26 July 1982.[20] These regulations oblige the landlord of a controlled dwelling to register particulars of the tenancy and the dwelling with the housing authority.[21] According to the Rent Tribunal's Annual Report and Accounts 1990, 10,426 formerly controlled dwellings had by the end of that year been registered throughout the country, of which 5,308 were situate in Dublin.

The regulations require registration of particulars of changes in the rent, the name of the tenant and other matters.[22] A charge of £20 is payable on the first occasion a new rent is notified to the housing authority and a charge of

14. Ibid., section 24(1).
15. Ibid.
16. Ibid., section 24(3).
17. Ibid., section 24(4).
18. Ibid., section 24(5). Provision is made for the obtaining of extracts from the register and their use as evidence: Housing (Private Rented Dwellings) Act 1982 section 24(6)-(8).
19. Ibid., section 25(2).
20. Housing (Private Rented Dwellings) Regulations 1982, article 2. Minor amendments to the 1982 Regulations have been made by the Housing (Private Rented Dwellings) (Amendment) Regulations 1983, SI No. 286 of 1983.
21. Ibid., article 5 as amended by the Housing (Private Rented Dwellings) (Amendment) Regulations 1983, article 3.
22. Ibid., articles 6 and 7 as amended by the Housing (Private Rented Dwellings) (Amendment) Regulations 1983, article 4.

£10 on each occasion thereafter.[23] The regulations also require a landlord to provide his tenant with a rent book within one month of registration of the tenancy.[24] The rent book must set out in clearly legible writing the name and address of the landlord and his agent, if any; the address of the dwelling; and the rent payable.[25] It must also include a note in the form set out in the schedule to the regulations advising the tenant (*inter alia*) that the landlord may only increase the rent by agreement with the tenant or by order of the court; that a tenant who has difficulty in paying an increase in rent may be eligible for a rent allowance from the Department of Social Welfare; and that a landlord may not evict a tenant without having obtained a court order.[26] Each payment of rent and the period covered by it must be recorded by the landlord or his agent on production by the tenant of the rent book.[27] Particulars of changes in the rent or the name and address of the landlord or his agent must also be recorded.[28]

Enforcement of regulations Contravention of the regulations made under sections 24, 25 and 26 of the 1982 Act is an offence; and the offender is liable on summary conviction to a fine not exceeding £500.[29] Responsibility for their enforcement rests with the housing authority.[30]

23. Ibid., article 9.
24. Ibid., article 10(1). It seems likely that this requirement of a rent book will in the future be extended to virtually all dwellings in the private rented sector: see *A Plan for Social Housing* published by the Department of the Environment in February 1991.
25. Ibid., article 10(2).
26. Ibid.
27. Ibid., article 10(4).
28. Ibid., article 10(3).
29. Housing (Private Rented Dwellings) Act 1982, section 27(1).
30. Ibid., section 27(3).

SEVEN

Proceedings before the Rent Tribunal, rent officers and the High Court under the 1983 Act

The composition of the Rent Tribunal The Rent Tribunal was set up under the Housing (Private Rented Dwellings) (Amendment) Act 1983. Its purpose is to hear applications to fix the terms of tenancies of controlled dwellings, a jurisdiction formerly exercised by the District Court under the Housing (Private Rented Dwellings) Act 1982. Its members are appointed by the Minister for the Environment; and include a chairman and so many vice-chairmen and ordinary members as the minister, with the consent of the Minister for the Public Service, considers necessary.[1] Disqualified from membership are members of the Dáil and Seanad, local authorities and European Assembly.[2] Officers of the Minister for the Environment may be appointed to assist the tribunal in the performance of its functions.[3]

The tribunal sits in divisions of three persons. The chairman of each division is either the chairman of the tribunal or one of the vice-chairmen. The tribunal's practice is to include in its divisions at least one person with valuing experience and, where possible, a lawyer.

Disclosure requirements The 1983 Act makes strict provision in section 14 for the disclosure by a member of the tribunal of any beneficial interest in the dwelling, the subject of an application or appeal, or any other interest in the application or appeal which would be likely to influence him. The nature of the interest must be disclosed to the tribunal; the member concerned must take no part in the discussion on, or consideration of, the case; nor may he vote or act as a member of the tribunal in dealing with the case.[4] Likewise,

1. Housing (Private Rented Dwellings) (Amendment) Act 1983, section 2(2) and (3). According to the tribunal's Annual Report and Accounts 1990 there were at the end of that year, in addition to the chairman, six vice-chairmen and six ordinary members.
2. Ibid., section 3.
3. Ibid., section 2(4).
4. Ibid., section 14(1).

where an officer of the tribunal has an interest in the case, he must disclose it to the tribunal and comply with any directions the tribunal may give in relation to the matter.[5] A person is regarded as having a beneficial interest in a dwelling if he or his spouse is the landlord or tenant of the dwelling; or if he or his spouse or a nominee is a member of a company or other body which is the landlord of the dwelling; or if he or his spouse is in partnership with, or in the employment of, a person who is the landlord or tenant of the dwelling.[6] But if the interest of the person, or his company or other body, is so remote or insignificant that it cannot reasonably be regarded as likely to influence him, he will not be regarded as having a disqualifying interest.[7] Failure to comply with section 14 by a person who has a disqualifying interest will render the outcome of the case under consideration invalid and the case will have to be decided again.[8] Moreover, a person who has a beneficial interest in a dwelling and fails to comply with a requirement of section 14 is guilty of an offence and is liable on summary conviction to a fine not exceeding £500.[9] A member of the tribunal who is convicted of such an offence ceases to be a member.[10]

The work of the tribunal[11] In the period from its establishment on 2 August 1983[12] until the end of 1984 the tribunal received 1,073 applications to fix the terms of tenancies. In 1985 the number of applications declined to 367, as it did in 1986 (134), and in 1987 (111). This trend was reversed in 1988 when the number of applications rose to 187, and in 1989 the number rose again to 247. In 1990 the tribunal received 205 applications. The resurgence in the tribunal's workload is attributable to the number of applications for the review of terms previously fixed by the District Court or the tribunal. In 1990 almost 80% of the total applications were applications for review.

Not surprisingly most of the applications to the tribunal relate to dwellings in Dublin. In 1990 79% of applications related to dwellings in the Dublin area and 7.3% related to dwellings in the Cork area. Of the dwellings in respect of which determinations were made during 1990, 156 were houses (81% of the total), 13 were self-contained flats (8% of the total) and 22 were non self-contained flats (11% of the total).

5. Ibid., section 14(4).
6. Ibid., section 14(5).
7. Ibid., section 14(6).
8. Ibid., section 14(9) and (10).
9. Ibid., section 14(7).
10. Ibid., section 14(8).
11. See the tribunal's seven annual reports published to date.
12. By the Rent Tribunal (Date of Establishment) Order 1983, SI No. 220 of 1983.

The initiation of an application Procedure before the Rent Tribunal is dealt with in the Housing (Rent Tribunal) Regulations 1983.[13] An application to fix the terms of a tenancy may be made by either the landlord or the tenant, but must be in writing on an application form provided by the tribunal.[14] One month's notice must be given to the other party.[15] The tribunal must acknowledge receipt of an application and notify the respondent, sending him a copy of the application and indicating whether a request has been made for an oral hearing.[16]

The tribunal may require the applicant to furnish information relating to the application and to furnish evidence to verify any particulars or information given by him.[17] Neglect or refusal to give the information or evidence sought may result in the tribunal determining the application without the information or evidence.[18] Where a written submission is made to the tribunal in relation to an application, the tribunal must send a copy of it to the other party if of the opinion that it is of significance to the determination of the application.[19] Where the tribunal is of the opinion that the determination of the application is being unnecessarily delayed by one or both of the parties, it may determine the application on the basis of the information before it or regard the application as having been abandoned.[20] If it regards the application as having been abandoned, it must notify the parties accordingly.[21]

Oral hearings Since its establishment the tribunal has determined many cases coming before it by oral hearing which may be requested by either party to an application.[22] The request must be made in writing and, if made

13. SI No. 222 of 1983. However, failure or neglect to comply with the Regulations will not necessarily prevent the Tribunal from determining an application: Housing (Rent Tribunal) Regulations 1983, article 5(3).
14. Housing (Private Rented Dwellings) (Amendment) Act 1983, section 5(1) and Housing (Rent Tribunal) Regulations 1983, article 5(1). Most applications to the tribunal are made by landlords: the records show that since its establishment applications by landlords ranged over the years from 93 to 99% of the total.
15. Housing (Private Rented Dwellings) (Amendment) Act 1983, section 5(5).
16. Housing (Rent Tribunal) Regulations 1983, article 5(2).
17. Ibid., article 7(1)(a).
18. Ibid., article 7(1)(b).
19. Ibid., article 7(3). A copy of any consultant's report commissioned by the tribunal must also be sent to each party: Housing (Rent Tribunal) Regulations 1983, articles 7(4) and 15.
20. Ibid., article 7(1)(c).
21. Ibid., article 7(2).
22. Ibid., article 8(1). In general there has been a decline in the use of oral hearings. According to the tribunal's annual reports, 62.4% of cases were determined by oral hearing during the period 1983/84; 66.2% were so determined in the year 1985; 60% in

by the applicant, must be made at the time of making the application; if made by the respondent, it must be made not later than 14 days from the date of notice to him of receipt of the application.[23] If a request is made, the tribunal must hold an oral hearing.[24] It must give each party not less than 14 days' notice of the time and place of the hearing or such shorter notice as may be accepted by them.[25] The tribunal may alter the time and place of the hearing in which case it must give each party not less than seven days' notice of the new time and place or such shorter notice as may be accepted by them.[26] If neither party requests an oral hearing, no hearing will be held unless the tribunal considers it necessary to do so.[27]

The conduct of the oral hearing lies in the discretion of the tribunal.[28] It must, however, conduct the hearing without undue formality.[29] It must permit any party to appear in person or to be represented by another person and it must, if it thinks fit, hear any person who is not a party to the application.[30] A party to an application may make an opening statement, call witnesses, question witnesses called by the other party, give evidence on his own behalf and address the tribunal at the close of the evidence.[31] The tribunal may take account of any written submissions made to it prior to the hearing and may admit any written statement as *prima facie* evidence of any fact whenever it thinks it is just and proper to do so.[32] A person who knowingly gives false or misleading information to the tribunal in the course of the determination of a case is guilty of an offence.[33] If after due notice a party to an application fails to appear, the tribunal may determine the application or adjourn the hearing.[34]

A feature of Rent Tribunal cases is the practice of the tribunal to carry out an inspection of the dwelling under consideration. Section 17(1) of the 1983 Act empowers a member of the tribunal or a person authorised by it to enter and inspect a dwelling the subject of an application or appeal. According to the tribunal's 1983/84 report, 'Prior to the determination of the case, each dwelling is inspected by all members of the division as far as is reasonably

the year 1986; and 57% in the year 1987. But in 1988 the proportion of cases determined by oral hearing fell to 38%; in 1989 the proportion fell to 32% and in 1990 the proportion was 37%.

23. Ibid., article 8(1) and (2).
24. Ibid., article 8(3).
25. Ibid., article 9(1).
26. Ibid., article 9(2).
27. Ibid., article 8(4).
28. Ibid., article 10(1).
29. Ibid., article 10(1)(a).
30. Ibid., article 10(1)(b) and (c).
31. Ibid., article 10(2).
32. Ibid., article 10(3).
33. Housing (Private Rented Dwellings) (Amendment) Act 1983, section 16(1).
34. Housing (Rent Tribunal) Regulations 1983, article 10(5).

practicable, and in any event, by the member with valuing experience. The Tribunal finds that this inspection of dwellings is a very valuable aid in the determination of applications and one for which there is no adequate substitute.'[35]

Legal representation and costs In most cases decided by oral hearing one or both of the parties has legal representation.[36] Under the regulations, if a party intends to be legally represented at the oral hearing, he must give not less than seven days' notice to the other party and to the tribunal.[37] And he will not be entitled to legal representation unless the tribunal is satisfied that he has complied with these requirements.[38] A party to whom a notification has been given is not, however, obliged to notify the other party of his own intention to have legal representation.[39]

The costs and expenses of an application lie in the discretion of the tribunal, and may be awarded to either party having regard to all the circumstances of the case including means.[40] Their amount is determined by the tribunal and is recoverable as a simple contract debt.[41] As a general rule the tribunal makes the landlord liable for the tenant's costs and expenses of an application.

Withdrawal of an application An applicant may withdraw an application by giving notice of withdrawal to the tribunal and to the respondent.[42] But where the parties have been notified by the tribunal of the time and place of an oral hearing the notice of withdrawal must be given not less than seven days before the hearing.[43]

Rent officers The Minister for the Environment is empowered, under section 6 of the 1983 Act, to direct by order that all applications to fix the terms of tenancies of controlled dwellings are to be made to housing authorities for determination by rent officers. To date no such order has been

35. Annual Report and Accounts 1983/84, p. 2.
36. In 1983-4 there was legal representation in only 53.3% of the cases determined by oral hearing; this figure rose to 71.6% in 1985, to 80% in 1986, and to 96.6% in 1987. However, in recent years the proportion of cases in which there was legal representation appears to have stabilised. In 1988 the proportion was 71%; in 1989 it was 75%; and in 1990 it was 68%.
37. Housing (Rent Tribunal) Regulations 1983, article 11(1).
38. Ibid., article 11(3).
39. Ibid., article 11(2).
40. Ibid., article 12(1) as substituted by Housing (Rent Tribunal) Regulations 1983 (Amendment) Regulations 1988, article 3.
41. Ibid., article 12(2) as substituted by Housing (Rent Tribunal) Regulations 1983 (Amendment) Regulations 1988, article 3.
42. Ibid., article 5(4).
43. Ibid.

made; but housing authorities will be required to appoint rent officers, if and when an order is made.[44] Thereafter either the landlord or tenant of a controlled dwelling may apply to the housing authority in whose functional area the dwelling is situated to have the terms of the tenancy fixed by a rent officer.[45] Either party may appeal against the determination to the Rent Tribunal.[46] The provisions of section 14 of the 1983 Act as to the disclosure of qualifying interests also apply to rent officers. If a rent officer has an interest in the dwelling the subject of the application, or has any other interest in the application which would be likely to influence him in determining the terms of the tenancy, he must inform the manager of the housing authority and must neither make nor seek to influence the determination of the tenancy.[47]

Appeals from the rent officer to the Rent Tribunal As we have seen, an appeal lies from the determination of a rent officer to the Rent Tribunal. If the terms of the tenancy are varied by the tribunal, the terms as so varied are binding on the parties.[48] And if the rent fixed on appeal by the tribunal is less than that fixed by the rent officer, the tenant may either deduct the excess paid by him from his rent or sue to recover it as a simple contract debt.[49] Particulars of the rent determined by the rent officer may be registered even though an appeal is made from his decision.[50] On hearing an appeal from a determination of a rent officer, the tribunal is empowered to order one party to pay the other an amount not exceeding the difference between the old rent and the new rent for the period from the date of the determination of the rent officer to the date of the fixing of the terms by the tribunal.[51] Payment is to be made in such manner and over such period as the tribunal may direct having regard to all the circumstances of the case.[52] The decision of the tribunal is final and no appeal lies against it except to the High Court on a question of law.[53]

Appeals to the High Court Where the terms of a tenancy are fixed by the tribunal in the first instance, or on appeal from a determination of a rent officer, either party may, under section 13 of the 1983 Act, appeal to the High

44. Housing (Private Rented Dwellings) (Amendment) Act 1983, section 6(2).
45. Ibid., section 5(1).
46. Ibid., section 11(1).
47. Ibid., section 14(2).
48. Ibid., section 11(2).
49. Ibid., section 11(3).
50. Ibid., section 11(4).
51. Ibid., section 12(1)(b).
52. Ibid., section 12(2).
53. Ibid., section 12(3).

Court on a question of law. The appeal must be made within three months of the tribunal's determination or such longer period as the High Court may allow.[54] In addition, the tribunal may request the minister to refer a question of law to the High Court in which event the minister may be represented at the hearing.[55] Every appeal to the High Court under the Act is to be brought by special summons which is to be served on all parties to the decision of the tribunal.[56]

The function of the High Court in determining an appeal was considered by Gannon J in *Quirke v Folio Homes Ltd.*[57] 'The appeal before this Court,' he held,[58] 'can only proceed on the basis of the facts presented to the Tribunal as shown in the evidence given to this Court. As a determination of the Tribunal is essentially a matter of the opinion of the Tribunal as to what is just and proper upon the information put before it this Court can only investigate whether or not the material before the Tribunal was such that the Tribunal could reasonably arrive at the opinion in respect of which this appeal has been brought.' These *dicta* of Gannon J may usefully be compared with the decision of the the Supreme Court in *Rahill v Brady*[59] on the meaning of 'a point of law' for the purposes of an appeal from the District Court by way of case stated under section 2 of the Summary Jurisdiction Act 1857 as amended by section 51 of the Courts (Supplemental Provisions) Act 1961. In *Rahill* the respondent obtained occasional licences in the District Court authorising him to sell intoxicating liquor at a livestock mart in the town of Cavan in the month of April 1969 when sales of cattle and pigs were to be held. The licences were granted under the Intoxicating Liquor Act 1962 which enabled the District Justice to grant the licences if satisfied that a 'special event' was to be held at the premises. The appellants appealed by case stated to the High Court on the ground that the decision of the District Justice was wrong on 'a point of law' in that the sales in the mart were not 'special events' within the meaning of the Intoxicating Liquor Act 1962. The High Court and the Supreme Court on appeal held that the issue to be determined did involve a point of law and that the bi-weekly sales of cattle and pigs at a place normally used for that purpose were not 'special events'. Budd J, in the Supreme Court, was emphatic in his view[60] that:

> A decision on such a matter is not a decision on a question of fact only;

54. Ibid., section 13(1).
55. Ibid., section 13(2).
56. RSC O. 112.
57. Unreported judgment of the High Court (Gannon J) delivered 4 March 1985.
58. At p. 7 of the judgment.
59. [1971] IR 69.
60. Expressed at pp. 85-86 of the report.

> it is a decision on a mixed question of law and fact. The construction of a statute is involved. No doubt there may be borderline cases in which it might be thought the proper course was to accept the view formed by the District Justice as to the nature of the event, but that does not alter the main principle that the exercise of his discretion is open to review. A large number of cases of this kind will clearly fall on one side or the other of the line and it is well within the competence of the higher courts to examine the District Justice's finding in order to ascertain whether there is adequate evidence to support it and whether the decision has been made on a right and proper basis. Obviously, for example, a decision made without adequate evidence or reasons to support it should be set aside.

These words of Budd J may be taken as authority for the proposition that the High Court will review the decision of a tribunal on a point or question of law where the decision is based on inadequate evidence or reasons. Such an approach is consistent with the judgment of Gannon J in the *Quirke* case and may be thought to be in line with the practice of the Court of Appeal in England where it has been said[61] that:

> There are many tribunals from which an appeal lies only on a 'point of law': and we always interpret the provision widely and liberally.

61. By Lord Denning MR in *Instrumatic Ltd v Supabrase Ltd* [1969] 1 WLR 519, 521.

EIGHT

Recovery of possession

A landlord who, without an order of the court, evicts a tenant whose tenancy is protected by the Rent Acts will be liable in damages.[1] The court may, if necessary, grant an injunction to restrain a landlord from re-entering a controlled dwelling.[2] But where the tenant committed a nuisance, which would have entitled the landlord to an order for possession, the court refused an injunction and gave a decree for a small amount of damages.[3]

The recovery of possession of a controlled dwelling other than one subject to a service or temporary convenience letting is regulated by section 16 of the 1982 Act. An order for possession may be granted where the landlord satisfies any one of the five criteria set out in section 16(1) and the court considers it reasonable to make the order. When considering whether it is reasonable to make an order for recovery of possession the court is to have regard to the extent, if any, to which the conduct of the landlord contributed to the existence of the grounds upon which he relies in support of his application.[4] A local authority is not subject to the restrictions on recovery of possession if the dwelling is reasonably required for the purpose of the execution of its powers, functions and duties.[5]

The requirement of reasonableness Before making an order for possession section 16(1) requires that the court consider the granting of the order to be reasonable. This requirement was also imposed under the old legislation;[6] and, in practice, the courts have taken a pragmatic approach in applying it. Thus it was held in *Noonan v Reddy*[7] that it would not be reasonable to order possession where the landlord continued to accept rent in the knowledge that the tenant was in breach of a covenant against subletting. In *Fitzsimons v*

1. *Cruise v Terrell* [1922] 1 KB 664.
2. *O'Shaughnessy v Harrington* 67 ILTR 189.
3. *Brophy v Robertson* [1937] Ir Jur Rep 16.
4. Housing (Private Rented Dwellings) Act 1982, section 16(2).
5. Ibid., section 16(3). See pp. 21-3 ante in relation to the application of the Acts to the state.
6. See section 29(1) of the Rent Restrictions Act 1960.
7. 59 ILTR 131.

Parker[8] the tenant held under a lease which provided that the premises were to be used as a 'private dwelling only'. However, the tenant used the dwelling for the business of breeding and boarding dogs over a long period of time. The landlord was aware of this user and in some measure he acquiesced in it. The court held that it would not be reasonable to make an order for possession without giving the tenant an opportunity of discontinuing the user. And where the breach of covenant complained of by the landlord had been remedied, it was held in *Hardwicke Ltd v Murphy (No. 2)*[9] that it would not be reasonable to make an order. Nor, it was held in *Westport Harbour Commissioners v McBride*,[10] would it be reasonable to make an order where the landlord sought possession in order to let the premises to a new tenant who would undertake a line of business which the old tenant refused. If the landlord is required to pay compensation to the tenant in order to obtain his decree, the amount of compensation will be taken into account in determining whether it is reasonable to grant an order for possession.[11]

The grounds for an order for possession The grounds on which a landlord can recover possession under section 16 can be divided into two categories: cases where the tenant, or some person residing in the dwelling, is in some way in default, for example, where the rent has not been paid; and cases where there is no fault on the part of the tenant, but the landlord seeks possession to fulfil some object of his own, for example, the use of the dwelling as a residence for himself or some person bona fide residing with him. The grounds set out in section 16(1)(a) to (c) fall into the first category. The grounds set out in (d) and (e) fall into the second. Where the landlord recovers possession to secure some objective of his own, that is to say, where he recovers possession on one of the grounds under section 16(1)(d) or (e), he is required by section 16(1) to pay such sum as the court considers reasonable to meet the expenses incurred by the tenant in quitting the dwelling, together with a sum not exceeding three years' rent of alternative accommodation which is reasonably suited to the residential and other needs of the tenant, his spouse and his family bona fide residing with him.

It is not altogether clear what is intended by requiring a landlord to pay 'a sum not exceeding three years' rent of alternative accommodation'. Under the 1960 Act a landlord was also sometimes required to pay compensation to the tenant before being granted an order for possession.[12] Commenting on

8. [1949] Ir Jur Rep 59.
9. 85 ILTR 109.
10. [1931] L J Ir 50.
11. *Merchant Banking Ltd v O'Beirne* [1964] IR 370.
12. See section 29(1)(i) and (j) of the 1960 Act as amended by section 9 of the 1967 Act.

this requirement, Davitt P In *Merchant Banking Ltd v O'Beirne*[13] made the following observation:

> What the Legislature contemplated was, I think, an amount which would be in the nature of a compromise in which each party would be giving away something in order to find a just solution of the difficulty occasioned by conflicting rights and interests.

The compensation payable under section 16(1) is calculated by reference to the evidence of a valuer as to rents currently being obtained for accommodation which the court regards as reasonably suited to the tenant's residential and other needs. Having been so guided as to the amount of the rent, the court then has to determine how many years' rent will have to be paid to the tenant. In the absence of special circumstances, the court will usually require that the amount of the rent for the full period of three years be paid. Certainly, where the landlord is agreeable to pay this, or an even larger amount, it will be easier to convince the court that the granting of an order for possession is reasonable.

The court may grant an order for the recovery of possession where 'rent lawfully due by the tenant has not been paid' An order for possession should not be made until the court determines affirmatively that the rent due from the tenant has not been paid. So where there was a question as to the amount payable, it was held that possession should not be ordered pending its determination.[14] The rent was held to be lawfully due where the landlord sought possession, having previously obtained a judgment for the rent.[15] In *Cornwall v Ramplin*[16] it was held that the tenant was bound by the amount of the rent set out in an earlier District Court decree in ejectment for overholding, and could not go behind the decree in order to dispute the amount. Where, in *Boyle v Fitzsimons*,[17] the rent was in arrears, an order for possession was made subject to a stay; and it was further ordered that the order for possession was not to issue if the rent was paid before expiry of the stay. But where the tenant never paid the rent punctually an order for possession was granted.[18]

13. [1964] IR 370, 373.
14. *Dun Laoghaire UDC v Moran* [1921] 2 IR 404; 56 ILTR 12.
15. *Farrelly v Tierney* 67 ILTR 263; [1933] L J Ir 191.
16. 68 ILTR 223. See also *Kinsella v Connor* 76 ILTR 141.
17. [1926] IR 378; 60 ILTR 122. See also *Urkwickee v Gutkin* 55 ILTR 39.
18. *Chartres v Muldoon* 57 ILTR 102.

The court may grant an order for the recovery of possession where 'any other obligation under the tenancy has not been fulfilled' Two old cases concern licensed premises which were subject to the Rent Acts. The tenant, in *Gildea v Conway*,[19] was bound under his agreement to keep the premises in repair, to keep up the licence and to do no act which would imperil the licence. Having acquired other licensed premises in the same town, he had virtually closed the demised premises and starved it of its trade. These actions were, it was held, a breach of the spirit of the tenancy agreement entitling the court to refuse the tenant the benefit of the 1915 Rent Act. Another tenant of licensed premises, in *Folan v Lee*,[20] was bound by a covenant not to do or suffer any act whereby the licence might be liable to forfeiture, or have a conviction recorded thereon, or the renewal thereof withheld. He was convicted of an offence against the licensing laws but the conviction was not recorded on the licence. It was held that an order for possession should be made on the ground (*inter alia*) that an obligation of the tenancy had been broken.

In *In re Drew*[21] the tenant was held to be excluded from the protection of the 1923 Act where he had broken one of the conditions of his tenancy by allowing himself to be adjudicated bankrupt. An order for possession was made in *Keller v O'Neill*[22] where the tenant in breach of covenant sublet the premises, less one room, as a furnished house. So too in *O'Leary v O'Flynn*[23] where the lease provided that 'the tenant shall use the premises as a dwelling-house only' and the tenant sublet two portions of the dwelling and occupied the remainder herself. Where, in *Powerscourt v Doran*,[24] the tenant was in breach of a covenant to repair, the court granted a decree for possession subject to a stay on the tenant's undertaking to complete the required repairs. But in *Noonan v Reddy*,[25] where the breach of obligation relied upon by the landlord in his claim for possession was committed with his full knowledge, and he continued to accept rent with this knowledge, it was held that it would not be reasonable to make an order for possession.

The court may grant an order for the recovery of possession where 'any person (being the tenant or any person residing in the dwelling) has been guilty of conduct which the court is satisfied is a nuisance or annoyance to the landlord or his agent or to adjoining occupiers' The reference to

19. 53 ILTR 166.
20. [1926] IR 87; 59 ILTR 129.
21. [1929] IR 504; 63 ILTR 142.
22. 60 ILTR 83.
23. [1949] Ir Jur Rep 21.
24. [1941] Ir Jur Rep 83. See also *Strecker v Hayden* 76 ILT & SJ 132.
25. 59 ILTR 131.

'adjoining occupiers' is limited to those in actual occupation.[26] So, for example, a decree for possession was granted in *Bermingham v McNeill*[27] where the tenant persisted in playing his radio late at night causing annoyance to the other occupants of the house. But the nuisance or annoyance relied upon by the landlord does not have to be connected with the use of the demised dwelling.[28] A decree for possession was granted in *Patterson v Culhane*[29] where the tenant's conduct in preventing the landlord from letting an adjoining premises was held to be '*ejusdem generis* with conduct which is a nuisance to an adjoining occupier'. A broad view of the ground was also taken in *O'Connor v Byrne*[30] where the mere letting of a house situate in a good residential area in separate tenements was held to be a nuisance and annoyance to adjoining occupiers. But it seems that acts of nuisance or annoyance committed under a bona fide claim of right may not sustain a claim for ejectment.[31] Where the nuisance was such as would have entitled the landlord to a decree for possession and he forcibly deprived the tenant of possession, it was held in *Brophy v Robertson*[32] that the tenant was entitled to damages but not to an order restoring him to possession.

The court may grant an order for the recovery of possession where 'any person (being the tenant or any person residing in the dwelling) has used the dwelling or allowed it to be used for any immoral or illegal purpose (whether or not the person has been convicted of so using it or allowing it to be so used)' An order for possession was made in *Folan v Lee*[33] where the tenant of licensed premises was convicted of concealing illicit spirits on which the duty had not been paid though the conviction was not recorded on the licence.

The court may grant an order for the recovery of possession where 'the condition of the dwelling has, in the opinion of the court, deteriorated owing to acts of waste by, or the neglect or default of the tenant or any person residing in the dwelling' It seems that a court may make an order for possession when the condition of the dwelling has deteriorated through the neglect of the tenant even though there has been no breach of the tenancy agreement.[34] Considering that many controlled dwellings have been noted

26. *Hall v Nulty* 71 ILTR 198.
27. 70 ILT & SJ 293.
28. *Hall v Nulty*, supra.
29. 50 ILTR 116.
30. [1945] Ir Jur Rep 30.
31. *Hall v Nulty*, supra.
32. [1937] Ir Jur Rep 16. Cf. *O'Shaughnessy v Harrington* 67 ILTR 189.
33. [1926] IR 87; 59 ILTR 129.
34. *Lowe v Landrum* 156 Estates Gazette 423.

to be in a poor condition, it is perhaps surprising that there are not many applications to the District Court for orders for possession on this ground. The explanation may lie in the fact that the poor condition of these dwellings is frequently as much attributable to default on the part of the landlord as on the part of the tenant; and that, in these circumstances, it would be very difficult to persuade a court that it would be reasonable to make an order.

The court may grant an order for the recovery of possession where 'the dwelling is bona fide required by the landlord for occupation as a residence for himself or any person bona fide residing or to reside with him The meaning of 'bona fide residing or to reside' with the landlord was considered in *Scully v Tomlinson.*[35] Here the landlord sought possession of a flat for use as a waiting room, consulting room and a bedroom for his son, a medical doctor. The son intended to engage a housekeeper to attend to his household requirements. He did not intend to take his meals with his parents who occupied the upper portion of the house in which the flat was situated. On these facts it was held that the landlord's son could not be described as a 'person bona fide residing with or (about) to reside with' the landlord.

The landlord who seeks possession must show that the premises are required 'for occupation as a residence.' He will not, therefore, obtain a decree for possession where the dwelling is required for business purposes.[36] Though where the dwelling was required for use partly as a dwelling and partly for business purposes, a landlord has been allowed to recover possession.[37]

Where there is more than one landlord, and a claim for possession is made on the ground that the landlord requires possession for his own occupation, then all the persons holding the landlord's interest must show that they intend to occupy the dwelling. Thus, in *McRory v McCrossan,*[38] a decree for possession was refused where three persons held the landlord's interest but only two of them intended to occupy the dwelling.

The court may grant an order for the recovery of possession where 'the dwelling is bona fide required by the landlord for occupation as a residence for a person in the wholetime employment of the landlord' 'Wholetime employment' means actual and not prospective employment.[39]

35. 88 ILT & SJ 262.
36. *Laird v Graves* 55 ILTR 55.
37. *Lyons v Lyons* [1935] Ir Jur Rep 9 applied in *Sheppard v Collins (No. 2)* [1942] Ir Jur Rep 55.
38. 83 ILTR 42. See also *Breslin v D'Alton* 87 ILT & SJ 318.
39. *Johnston v Curran* 55 ILT & SJ 4; *Cromer v Murray* [1932] L J Ir 101.

The court may grant an order for the recovery of possession where 'the dwelling is bona fide required by the landlord in the interests of good estate management' Good estate management denotes something more than that possession is in the interest of the landlord; he has to show that his estate benefits. A good example is provided by *Gallagher v Earl of Leitrim*[40] where an application under the Landlord and Tenant Act 1931 for a new tenancy of a gatelodge, which had been used partly as a tailor's workshop and was situated at the main entrance to a residential demesne, was refused as not being consistent with good estate management. On the same ground, in *Hardwicke Ltd v Byrne*,[41] an order for possession was granted under the Rent Restrictions Act 1960 of a dwelling used in part for business purposes. But it was held that, in determining the amount of compensation payable by the landlord, the court could, though bound to regard the premises as a dwelling, have regard to the fact that a business had been carried on in it.

The court may grant an order for the recovery of possession where 'the landlord requires vacant possession to carry out a scheme of development of property which includes the dwelling and has planning permission for the scheme' 'Development' has the meaning assigned to it by section 3 of the Local Government (Planning and Development) Act 1963: 'the carrying out of any works on, in, or under land or the making of any material change in the use of any structures or other land'. That there must be a 'scheme of development' implies that the development must be part of an overall plan or purpose. A useful comparison may be made with section 17(2)(a) of the Landlord and Tenant (Amendment) Act 1980 which prevents a tenant from acquiring a new tenancy under that Act where (*inter alia*) 'the landlord requires vacant possession for the purpose of carrying out a scheme of development of the property which includes the tenement.' This provision is a re-enactment of section 22 of the Landlord and Tenant Act 1931 and the meaning of the phrase 'scheme of development' under that section was considered in *O'Reilly v Kevans*.[42] Here the tenant sought a new tenancy in a one storey shed or yard claiming that he used the premises for storing materials necessary for his business. The landlords, the trustees for the Loreto Convent, North Great George's Street, resisted the application on the grounds that they proposed to build a science laboratory on the site of the premises or to use the site for enlarging playground space available for children attending the school on adjoining property. The Circuit Court held that these proposals constituted a scheme of development within the meaning of the section.

40. [1948] Ir Jur Rep 23.
41. [1963] IR 52.
42. 69 ILTR 1.

'Planning permission' means either a full planning permission or outline planning permission.[43]

Order for possession obtained by misrepresentation If a landlord obtains an order for possession of a controlled dwelling by misrepresentation or concealment of material facts, then he may be ordered to pay the former tenant such sum as the court considers reasonable by way of compensation for damage or loss sustained by him as a result of the order.[44] It seems that the sum payable under this provision is compensatory in nature and not punitive.[45]

43. Housing (Private Rented Dwellings) Act 1982 section 16(4).
44. Ibid., section 19.
45. *Dowie v Leyburn* 70 ILT & SJ 338.

NINE

Court proceedings

The jurisdiction of the District Court under the 1982 Act A major innovation in the 1982 Act is the conferring by section 21 of jurisdiction on the District Court to hear and determine issues arising under part II of the Act. The jurisdiction is to be exercised by the judge for the time being assigned to the district in which the dwelling is situated.[1] In contrast, section 50 of the 1960 Act had limited the jurisdiction of the District Court by reference to the rateable valuation or annual rent of the dwelling, but otherwise conferred jurisdiction on the Circuit Court. Thus the District Court may now select the member of a deceased tenant's family to succeed to the tenancy; it may determine the amount to be paid by a landlord to a tenant who is quitting the dwelling as compensation for improvements; and it may grant an order for the recovery of possession. Prior to the 1983 Act the District Court also fixed the terms of the tenancy of a controlled dwelling, but this jurisdiction is now exercised by the Rent Tribunal.

Procedure in the District Court in cases under the 1982 Act Procedure in the District Court under the 1982 Act is regulated by the District Court [Housing (Private Rented Dwellings) Act 1982] Rules 1982.[2] These rules came into force on 22 September 1982. They prescribe the forms to be used for applications to the court under the Act and lay down scales for solicitors' costs.

Proceedings under the 1982 Act are generally initiated by the service of a notice. Section 4(1) of the Act provides that a notice may be served by delivering it to the person to whom it is addressed or by leaving it at the address at which he ordinarily resides, or by posting it to that address in a prepaid registered letter. For the purpose of service of notices a company is deemed to be ordinarily resident at its registered office and every other body corporate or unincorporated body is deemed to be ordinarily resident at its principal office or place of business.[3] A notice must be served at least one month before the sitting of the court to which it has been made returnable.[4]

1. Housing (Private Rented Dwellings) Act 1982, section 21(2).
2. SI No. 296 of 1982. 3. Housing (Private Rented Dwellings) Act 1982, section 4(2).
4. District Court [Housing (Private Rented Dwellings) Act 1982] Rules 1982, r. 5(ii).

The original notice must be lodged with the District Court clerk at least seven days before the sitting.[5] Proof of service is by a statutory declaration endorsed on the original notice.[6] Where proceedings are brought in the Dublin Metropolitan District, the original and a copy of every notice intended for service must be lodged with the District Court clerk for insertion of a return date.[7]

One form under the 1982 Rules merits special attention—form 8. This is the form to be used where the applicant seeks to recover possession under section 16 of the 1982 Act. It would appear that form 8 should only be used where the tenant holds by virtue of the 1982 or the earlier Rent Acts, and should not be used if the tenancy is still a contractual one. In such a case the contractual tenancy should be terminated, usually by serving a notice to quit, before an order for possession may be made.[8] But if the tenant already holds by virtue of the Rent Acts and the landlord serves a notice to quit, the notice will not be regarded as recognising a new contractual tenancy.[9] Furthermore, section 20 of the 1982 Act provides that if the landlord of a controlled dwelling 'institutes proceedings for the recovery of possession of the dwelling, the acceptance of any sum purporting to be rent by the landlord for the period from the date of the institution of the proceedings to the date on which they are finally determined shall not prejudice his right (if any) to recover possession of the dwelling . . .'

The application of the 1982 Act in other courts While the 1982 Act and the rules made under it have simplified proceedings in relation to controlled dwellings, it must be remembered that the fundamental question whether or not a dwelling is controlled may still be raised in proceedings apart from those under the 1982 Act. The question could, for instance, be raised by way of defence to ejectment proceedings. These proceedings can be brought in any of the courts of first instance; and, it is submitted, that section 21 of the Act is no bar to a consideration by any court other than the District Court of the question whether the dwelling is controlled. Indeed, if section 21 were to be treated as a bar to, say, the consideration by the Circuit Court of a tenant's defence that his dwelling is controlled, this would effectively subvert the purpose of the 1982 Act: a landlord could circumvent the Act by simply bringing proceedings in the Circuit Court.

5. Ibid.
6. Ibid.
7. Ibid., r. 5(iii).
8. See *Nelligan v Culloty* [1931] LJ Ir 143 and *O'Connor v Fitzgerald* 91 ILTR 32.
9. *Murphy v Kinsella* 62 ILTR 62.

District Court ejectments The District Court Rules 1948 provide for three types of ejectment civil process: the civil process in ejectment for overholding, the civil process in ejectment against a permissive occupant and the civil process in ejectment for non-payment of rent. The court's jurisdiction in ejectments for overholding or non-payment of rent is limited to cases where the rent does not exceed £5,000 per annum.[10] In ejectments against permissive occupants the District Court exercises jurisdiction concurrently with the Circuit Court.[11]

The civil process in ejectment for overholding is required to be in form XXI set out in the schedule of forms in the District Court Rules.[12] The statutory basis for this type of ejectment is to be found in section 72 of the Landlord and Tenant Law Amendment Act (Ireland) 1860 (Deasy's Act) which provides that where a tenant of lands 'shall neglect or refuse to give possession of the same after the determination of his interest, either by notice to quit or otherwise, it shall be lawful for (the) landlord to proceed by civil bill ejectment against such tenant and such other person, if any, as shall be in the actual occupation of the said premises.' The landlord proceeding by ejectment civil process for overholding must, in short, prove the relationship of the landlord and tenant and its termination. This type of civil process is used where a periodic tenancy has been terminated by notice to quit or where a tenant remains in possession after the expiry of the term of his lease.

The civil process in ejectment against a permissive occupant is required to be in form XXIII.[13] This type of ejectment has its foundation in section 82 of the Civil Bill Courts (Ireland) Act 1851 which provides for civil bill ejectment proceedings against any person let into occupation or possession of land 'by permission, or as servant or caretaker, or as tenant strictly at will or by sufferance'. The section requires that a demand must be made by the owner, or his known agent or bailiff, of the occupier that he quit and deliver up possession of the premises.

The civil process in ejectment for non-payment of rent is required to be in form XXV.[14] This type of ejectment was established by section 52 of Deasy's Act which provides that such an ejectment will lie whenever 'a year's rent shall be in arrear in respect of lands held under any fee-farm grant, lease, or other contract of tenancy, or from year to year, and whether by writing or otherwise . . .' This ejectment does not lie where the tenancy is one less than from year to year, such as monthly or weekly tenancy.[15] A

10. Courts of Justice Act 1924, section 77 as amended by the Courts Act 1991, section 4.
11. Courts of Justice Act 1928, section 17.
12. DCR 1948, r. 169.
13. Ibid., r. 170
14. Ibid., r. 171
15. *O'Sullivan v Ambrose* 32 LR Ir 102.

notable disadvantage of the ejectment for non-payment of rent is that the defendant, or other person interested in the contract of tenancy, may apply to the court for an order of restitution on payment of the amount due for rent, arrears of rent and costs, within six months of the execution of the decree for possession.[16]

An ejectment civil process must under the District Court Rules specify the names of the landlord and of the tenant, a description of the premises and where they are situated and the rent at which they have been held.[17] Where the proceedings are grounded on the termination of the tenancy, the fact and means of termination must be set forth.[18] The civil process must be served on every person in actual possession of the premises as tenant or subtenant at least 15 clear days before the sitting of the court at which the civil process is made returnable.[19]

Special summary ejectments in the District Court Section 15 of the Summary Jurisdiction (Ireland) Act 1851 provides that possession of small dwellings may be recovered in summary proceedings. This procedure may be availed of to recover possession of any house or part of a house situate in any city, town, borough, or village, in which any fair or market is usually held, held by the tenant for any term not exceeding one month, where the tenancy has been terminated by notice to quit. The section applies to small dwellings in the Dublin Metropolitan District.[20] And under the Housing (Private Rented Dwellings) Act 1982[21] the section applies to a controlled dwelling, other than one subject to a service or temporary convenience letting, if its rateable valuation does not exceed £10, there being no limit in respect of the rent.

Proceedings under section 15 of the 1851 Act are instituted by summons made returnable for a sitting of the court for the court area in which the dwelling is situate.[22] The summons must be served on every person in possession as tenant or subtenant.[23] If the tenant fails to appear, or fails to show reasonable cause why possession should not be given, the court may issue a warrant for possession on proof of the holding, the time and manner

16. See sections 70 and 71 of the Landlord and Tenant Law Amendment Act (Ireland) 1860 and see DCR 1948, r. 179.
17. DCR 1948, r. 174.
18. Ibid.
19. Ibid., r. 173(1).
20. Summary Jurisdiction (Ireland) Act 1871, section 10.
21. Section 17(2).
22. See section 15 of the 1851 Act and DCR 1948, r. 25.
23. *Deasy v Hickey* 5 NIJR 209 and *R (Hennegan) v Justices of the County Cork* IR 9 CL 203.

of its termination and the title of the landlord if it accrued after the letting was made.[24] The District Judge may, however, instead of issuing a warrant immediately on the determination of the case, make an order requiring the defendant to deliver up possession within a limited time; and after the expiration of the time limited by the order he may issue a warrant.[25] Where the tenant appears at the hearing and undertakes in writing to deliver up possession within 14 days and to pay the rent and any arrears in the meantime, the District Judge may not issue a warrant until the expiration of the 14 days.[26] If the tenant is still in occupation after the 14 days, the warrant will issue forthwith.[27] A warrant issued under section 15 of the 1851 Act in respect of a controlled dwelling, other than one subject to a service or temporary convenience letting, remains in force for six months from its date of issue and for such further period as the court may direct.[28]

A summary procedure also exists to eject permissive occupants, that is to say, any person in possession of lands or premises by permission of the owner as servant, herdsman or caretaker. This 'caretaker's summons', as it is known, is issued under section 86 of the Landlord and Tenant Law Amendment (Ireland) Act 1860 (Deasy's Act).[29] Finally, there are summary procedures used to eject cottier tenants.[30] A cottier tenancy is defined in section 81 of Deasy's Act as a tenement consisting of a dwellinghouse or cottage let without land, or let with land not exceeding half an acre, at a rent not exceeding £5 a year for one month, or from month to month, or lesser period, and held under a written agreement, the landlord undertaking to keep the house or cottage in repair.

Ejectments in the Circuit Court The Circuit Court has jurisdiction in ejectment cases if the rateable valuation of the land does not exceed £200.[31] The Circuit Court Rules provide for four types of ejectment civil bill: the ejectment civil bill—permissive occupant; the ejectment civil bill for overholding; the ejectment civil bill—non-payment of rent; and the ejectment civil bill on the title. The first three of these civil bills correspond to their counterparts in the District Court, sharing the same statutory bases. The

24. Summary Jurisdiction (Ireland) Act 1851, section 15(3).
25. DCR 1948, r. 68(6).
26. Summary Jurisdiction (Ireland) Act 1851, section 15(4).
27. Ibid.
28. Housing (Private Rented Dwellings) Act 1982, section 17(1).
29. For a detailed outline of the procedure under section 86 of Deasy's Act see Woods, *The District Court Practitioner—Remedies* (Limerick, 1987), pp. 361-364; see also Wylie, *Irish Landlord and Tenant Law*, op. cit., paras 27.41-27.44.
30. See Woods, *A District Court Guide in Civil, Licensing and Family Law* (1977), pp. 61-4.
31. Section 22(1) of the Courts (Supplemental Provisions) Act 1961 and the third schedule as amended by the Courts Act 1981, section 2(1).

ejectment civil bill on the title, on the other hand, derives from section 79 of the Civil Bill Courts (Ireland) Act 1851 and section 1 of the Civil Bill Courts (Ireland) Act 1874. In practice it is used mainly to eject a tenant whose lease has been forfeited. But its use is not confined to these cases. It may, for example, be used to eject a tenant at will, the person allowed into possession rent free for an indeterminate period; or even, instead of an ejectment civil bill for overholding, to eject an overholding tenant.

Whichever form is used, the ejectment civil bill should contain a sufficient description of the property sought to be recovered and the place where it is situate.[32] In an ejectment for non-payment of rent or overholding the civil bill must specify the names of the landlord and of the tenant, the nature of the tenancy and the rent at which it was last held.[33] Where the proceedings are grounded on the determination of the tenancy, the fact of determination and the means by which it has been determined must be specified; and where proceedings are grounded on the non-payment of rent, the amount of the rent due after all fair and just allowances and the gale day up to which it is due must be specified.[34]

Service of the civil bill in all actions for the recovery of land, other than ejectment proceedings for non-payment of rent or for overholding, must be on every person in actual possession, or in receipt of the rents and profits, of the lands unless the court directs otherwise.[35] In proceedings for non-payment of rent or overholding only the person or persons in actual possession of the lands as tenant or under-tenant must be served.[36] In cases of vacant possession service may be effected by posting a copy of the civil bill on the door of the dwellinghouse or some other conspicuous part of the property; but in such a case, the judge must be satisfied that there was no person in actual possession, or in receipt of the rents or profits, upon whom service might have been effected before giving judgment for possession.[37] A person not named in or served with the civil bill may by leave of the judge appear and defend at the hearing.[38] The Rules also provide that a plaintiff in ejectment proceedings may make an application for summary judgment where the defendant has entered an appearance or defence;[39] but such applications are rare in practice.

Ejectments in the High Court Owing to the increased jurisdictions of the

32. CCR, 1950; O. 35, r. 1.
33. Ibid., O. 35, r. 2.
34. Ibid.
35. Ibid., O. 35, r. 3.
36. Ibid.
37. Ibid., O. 35, r. 4.
38. Ibid., O. 6, r. 12.
39. Ibid., O. 25.

District and Circuit Courts few cases of ejectment are dealt with in the High Court. Under the Rules of the Superior Courts a landlord seeking to recover possession of land against a tenant whose term has expired or been determined by notice to quit or seeking to recover possession for non-payment of rent may proceed by summary summons.[40] In other cases the landlord must proceed by plenary summons.[41] The summons must contain the description of the property sought to be recovered with reasonable certainty and must state the county and county district or the city or town and parish in which it is situated.[42] The requirements as to the persons to be served are similar to those in the Circuit Court.[43] If a defendant fails to enter an appearance to the summons, judgment can be obtained in default.[44] If the defendant enters an appearance to a claim brought by a summary summons, the plaintiff may bring a motion before the Master of the High Court for liberty to enter final judgment.[45] In uncontested cases the Master may deal with the matter summarily.[46] In contested cases he must transfer the case to the court list for hearing.[47] The court may then give liberty to enter final judgment, dismiss the action or adjourn the case for plenary hearing as if the case had been originated by plenary summons.[48] A plaintiff landlord who proceeds by plenary summons may, if the defendant does not deliver his defence within the prescribed time, obtain judgment in the Central Office.[49]

Appeals Appeals in civil matters lie from the District Court to the Circuit Court and the decision of the Circuit Court on appeal is final and conclusive.[50] An appeal to the Circuit Court is instituted by lodging a notice of appeal with the District Court clerk and serving a copy of the notice on the opposing party within 14 days from the date of the decision.[51] An application to extend time for lodgment and service of a notice of appeal may be granted by the District Court.[52] However, notice that an application is to be made to

40. RSC; O. 2, r. 1(2).
41. Ibid., O. 1, r. 6.
42. Ibid., O. 4, r. 6.
43. See RSC; O. 9, rr. 8-11.
44. See RSC; O. 13, rr. 4-6.
45. RSC; O. 37, r. 1.
46. Ibid., O. 37, r. 4.
47. Ibid., O. 37, r. 5.
48. Ibid., O. 37, r. 6.
49. Ibid., O. 27, r. 2.
50. The Courts of Justice Act 1924, section 84 as amended by the Courts of Justice Act 1936, section 57.
51. DCR 1948, r. 190 as amended by DCR 1955, r. 16.
52. See DCR 1948, r. 13 as substituted by DCR 1955, r. 5 and *State v Wade* 91 ILTR 76.

extend the time for an appeal should be served on the other side, and it has been suggested that the application should be made to the Circuit Court.[53]

Appeals in civil matters lie from the Circuit Court to the High Court whose decision on appeal is final and conclusive.[54] An appeal is instituted by service of a notice of appeal on every party directly affected by the appeal within ten days from the date on which the judgment or order appealed from was pronounced in open court.[55] An extension of time for an appeal may be granted by the Master of the High Court.[56] An appeal to the Supreme Court from a decision of the High Court is brought by a notice of appeal served on all parties directly affected by the appeal within 21 days from the passing and perfecting of the judgment or order appealed against.[57]

Powers of the court in ejectment proceedings relating to a controlled dwelling Where an order for the recovery of possession of a controlled dwelling is made, the District Court has a wide discretion in relation to the fixing of the date for possession. It may, at the time of the order or at any time before its execution, stay execution or postpone the date of possession for such period or periods as it thinks fit.[58] The court may also stay execution or postpone the date of possession subject to conditions.[59] And if the conditions are complied with, the court may discharge or vary the order.[60] Where execution is stayed or the date of possession postponed the court may grant further stays or postponements.[61] An application for a further stay while the tenant pursued a claim for a new tenancy under the Landlord and Tenant Act was, however, refused in *Pewris v Roche*.[62] The application may be made ex parte in a case of urgency.[63]

Costs Where an application was made to the District Court under the 1982 Act to fix the terms of a tenancy section 12(6) of the Act provided that the landlord was to be liable 'for the tenant's costs and expenses reasonably and necessarily incurred arising out of the application by the landlord'; the rule, though, was not an absolute one: the court might order otherwise 'on consideration of all the circumstances, including the means of the landlord

53. *State (O'Sullivan) v Buckley* 101 ILTR 152.
54. See Courts of Justice Act 1936, sections 38 and 39.
55. See O. 61 of the RSC.
56. RSC; O. 63, r. 1(5).
57. See O. 58 of the RSC.
58. Housing (Private Rented Dwellings) Act 1982, section 18(1).
59. Ibid.
60. Ibid.
61. Ibid., section 18(2).
62. 66 ILTR 152. See also *Stringer v Donovan* 54 ILTR 139.
63. Housing (Private Rented Dwellings) Act 1982, section 18(2).

and the tenant'. Apart from section 12(6), the 1982 Act is silent on the question of costs, as indeed is the 1983 Act. However, rule 14 of the District Court [Housing (Private Rented Dwellings) Act 1982] Rules does provide that the costs of proceedings under sections 15 and 16 of the 1982 Act (claims for compensation for improvements and for the recovery of possession) are to be in accordance with the scales set out in the schedule to the Rules and that the costs of proceedings not specifically provided for in the Rules may be measured under rule 67 of the District Court Rules 1948.[64] In ejectment cases solicitors' costs are determined in accordance with the scales of costs set out in the District Court (Costs) Rules 1990 as amended by the District Court (Costs) (Amendment) Rules 1990.[65] No provision is made in any of the rules for counsel's fees; but it would appear to be open to a District Justice in an appropriate case to certify for counsel under the District Court (Counsel's Fees) Rules 1973.[66]

64. See p. 56 ante in relation to costs in the Rent Tribunal.
65. SI Nos. 67 and 194 of 1990.
66. SI No. 39 of 1973.

TEN

Rent allowances for tenants

The Rent Tribunal in its 1990 report has observed that: 'The majority of tenants, in the cases determined, are old people in receipt of pensions, most of whom live on their own.'[1] In this context the importance of the availability of a rent allowance can be readily appreciated. According to the 1990 report, 425 tenants the terms of whose tenancies had been fixed by the tribunal were in receipt of rent allowances. This represents over one-fifth of tenants whose cases have come before the tribunal.

The statutory basis for the rent allowance is to be found in section 23 of the 1982 Act which empowers the Minister for Social Welfare, with the consent of the Minister for Finance, to make regulations for the payment of allowances to the tenants of controlled dwellings who suffer hardship by reason of the increases in the rents of their dwellings. The Social Welfare (Rent Allowance) Regulations 1991 (SI No. 208 of 1991) have been made under this section. These regulations came into operation on 18 July 1991 and consolidated the regulatory scheme relating to rent allowances.

Conditions for receipt of allowance A rent allowance is payable to a person who is entitled to retain possession as the tenant of a dwelling under section 9 of the 1982 Act and who satisfies the conditions as to means specified in the Regulations.[2] Before an allowance is payable the terms of the tenancy must be fixed by the court, Rent Tribunal or a rent officer and they must be set out in written form, signed by the landlord or his agent, and a copy furnished to the tenant.[3] In addition, the tenancy and particulars of the new rent for the dwelling must be registered with the housing authority.[4]

The amount of the allowance In the case of a married person whose weekly means do not exceed £110 or in the case of any other person whose weekly means do not exceed £64, the allowance is a weekly amount equal to the

1. See the Rent Tribunal's Annual Report and Accounts 1990, p. 6.
2. Social Welfare (Rent Allowance) Regulations 1991, article 5.
3. Ibid.
4. Ibid.

amount by which the rent (calculated as a weekly rent) fixed by the court, tribunal or rent officer exceeds the rent so calculated payable prior to 26 July 1982.[5] But if the old rent was less than £5.15, then the allowance is to be the amount by which the new rent exceeds £5.15.[6] 'Married person' is defined as 'a person whose spouse is (a) living with him, (b) wholly or mainly maintaining him, or (c) being wholly or mainly maintained by him'.[7]

If the means of a married person exceed £110, then the weekly allowance is reduced by 50 pence for each £1 of weekly means in excess of £110 and by £1 for each £1 of weekly means in excess of £120.[8] If the applicant is not married and his means exceed £64, then the allowance is reduced by 50 pence for each £1 of weekly means in excess of £64 and by £1 for each £1 of weekly means in excess of £69.[9] A rent allowance can also be claimed by the tenant in the event that he is ordered to pay compensation to the landlord under section 14 of the 1982 Act or section 12 of the 1983 Act.[10] But no allowance is payable where the amount of the allowance would be less than £1.[11]

The amount of the allowance may be reduced, or the entitlement to it extinguished, having regard to: (1) the income of any person other than the tenant, his spouse or children resident in the dwelling; or (2) the reasonable accommodation needs of the tenant, account being taken of the availability of suitable alternative accommodation, the length of his occupancy of the dwelling and his personal and family circumstances.[12] 'Children' are defined as 'persons who (a) are under the age of 18 years, or (b) are of or over the age of 18 years and under the age of 21 years, and are receiving full-time instruction by day at any university, college, school or other educational establishment'.[13]

Calculation of means The following items are taken into account when calculating the means of an applicant for a rent allowance.[14]

> (1) All cash income including the annual net cash value of any non-cash earnings derived from personal exertions and the actual or estimated amount of any income which the applicant may reasonably expect to receive as head of the household.

5. Social Welfare (Rent Allowance) Regulations 1991, article 6(1).
6. Ibid.
7. Ibid., article 3.
8. Ibid., article 6(2).
9. Ibid.
10. Ibid., article 6(4).
11. Ibid., article 6(7).
12. Ibid., article 6(5).
13. Ibid., article 6(6).
14. Ibid., article 7(1).

(2) The value of property belonging to the applicant (not being property personally used or enjoyed by him or a farm leased by him under a lease which has been certified by the Irish Land Commission to be bona fide and in accordance with sound land use practice) which is invested or otherwise put to profitable use or which, though capable of investment or profitable use, is not so invested or used: the yearly value of this property is calculated by taking 5% of the first £400 of the capital value of the property and 10% of the remainder.
(3) The yearly value of any advantage accruing to the applicant from the use or enjoyment of property (other than a domestic dwelling or a farm building owned and occupied or furniture and personal effects) and from the leasing of a farm under a lease which has been certified by the Irish Land Commission to be bona fide and in accordance with sound land use practice.
(4) The yearly value of any benefit or privilege enjoyed by the applicant.
(5) All income and the yearly value of all property of which the applicant has directly or indirectly deprived himself in order to qualify himself or his spouse for the allowance, or for the receipt of the allowance at a higher rate than he or his spouse would otherwise be entitled.

The following items are not taken into account when calculating means.[15]

(1) Child benefit.
(2) Orphan's (contributory) allowance, orphan's (non-contributory) pension and death benefit by way of orphan's pension.
(3) An allowance for the domiciliary care of handicapped children under the Health Act 1970.
(4) Family income supplement under Part IVA of the Social Welfare (Consolidation) Act 1981 inserted by section 13 of the Social Welfare Act 1984.
(5) Payments by a health board in respect of a child who is boarded out.
(6) Monies received from a charitable organisation.
(7) Income arising from casual employment by a health board as a home help.

In the case of a married couple, or a couple cohabiting as man and wife, the means of the applicant and his partner are aggregated and regarded as the means of the applicant.[16] But where there is an increase in benefit, allowance, pension or assistance paid under the Social Welfare (Consolidation) Act 1981 or under the Health Acts arising as part of a general increase in such benefits,

15. Ibid., article 7(1)(a).
16. Ibid., article 7(7).

allowances, pensions or assistance, then any portion of the increase which would result in a reduction in the amount of a rent allowance is to be disregarded.[17]

Claims Every claim for an allowance should be made to the Minister for Social Welfare in the prescribed way on a form obtainable from the Department of Social Welfare, Aras Mhic Dhiarmada, Store Street, Dublin 1. The claim should be made within three months from the date on which the applicant becomes entitled to the allowance.[18] So it should be made as soon as possible after the tenancy has been registered and the terms fixed by the tribunal and furnished to the tenant. If the claim is not made within three months, the applicant is disqualified from receiving payment for any period more than three months before the date on which the claim is made, unless there was good cause for failure to make the claim and an order is made extending the time.[19] An applicant must furnish such certificates, documents, information and evidence as may be required by the minister and must, if so required, attend at such office or place as the minister may direct.[20]

A claim for a rent allowance is dealt with by a deciding officer.[21] An appeal from his decision lies to an appeals officer.[22] The appeal must be made within 21 days.[23]

17. Ibid., article 8.
18. Ibid., article 13(1).
19. Ibid., article 13(2), (3), (4) and (5).
20. Ibid., article 11(1).
21. Social Welfare (Consolidation) Act 1981, section 111 as applied and modified by article 19 and the schedule to the Social Welfare (Rent Allowance) Regulations 1991.
22. Ibid., section 298 as applied and modified by article 19 and the schedule to the Social Welfare (Rent Allowance) Regulations 1991.
23. The procedure to be followed on the hearing of an appeal is set out in articles 4 to 9 and 11 to 16 of the Social Welfare (Insurance Appeals) Regulations 1952 (SI No. 376 of 1952).

Appendix

Housing (Private Rented Dwellings) (Amendment) Act, 1982

Number 6 of 1982

AN ACT TO PROVIDE, IN ACCORDANCE WITH THE EXIGENCIES OF THE COMMON GOOD, FOR A MEASURE OF SECURITY OF TENURE FOR THE TENANTS OF CERTAIN DWELLINGS, FOR THE RENTS OF SUCH DWELLINGS AND FOR THE EVENTUAL CESSER OF THE ENTITLEMENT OF SUCH TENANTS TO RETAIN POSSESSION OF SUCH DWELLINGS, TO PROVIDE FOR ALLOWANCES FOR CERTAIN TENANTS, FOR THE REGISTRATION OF RENTED DWELLINGS AND FOR STANDARDS FOR RENTED DWELLINGS AND TO PROVIDE FOR OTHER MATTERS CONNECTED WITH THE MATTERS AFORESAID. [21*st May*, 1982]

BE IT ENACTED BY THE OIREACHTAS AS FOLLOWS:

PART I
PRELIMINARY AND GENERAL

1.—(1) This Act may be cited as the Housing (Private Rented Dwellings) Act, 1982.

(2) This Act shall come into operation on such day as the Minister may appoint by order.

2. (1) In this Act, except where the context otherwise requires—

"the Court" means the District Court;

"dwelling" means a house let as a separate dwelling, or a part so let, of any house, whether or not the tenant shares with any other persons any portion thereof or any accommodation, amenity or facility in connection therewith;

"housing authority" means—

(*a*) in the case of a county, exclusive of any borough or urban district therein, the council of the county, (*b*) in the case of a county or other borough, the corporation of the borough, and

(*c*) in the case of an urban district, the council of the district,

and references to the functional area of a housing authority shall be construed accordingly;

"landlord" means the person for the time being entitled to receive (otherwise than as agent for another person) the rent payable in respect of a dwelling;

"the Minister" means the Minister for the Environment.

(2) A reference in this Act to a Part or a section is to a Part or a section of this Act unless it is indicated that reference to some other enactment is intended.

(3) A reference in this Act to a subsection, paragraph or other division is to the subsection, paragraph or other division of the provision in which the reference occurs, unless it is indicated that reference to some other provision is intended.

3.—The expenses incurred by the Minister in the administration of this Act shall, to such extent as may be sanctioned by the Minister for Finance, be paid out of moneys provided by the Oireachtas.

4.—(1) Where a notice or claim under this Act or any regulations made thereunder is to be given to or served on a person, it shall be addressed to him and shall be given to or served on him in some one of the following ways:

(*a*) where it is addressed to him by name, by delivering it to him;

(*b*) by leaving it at the address at which he ordinarily resides or, in a case in which an address for service has been furnished, at that address;

(*c*) by sending it by post in a prepaid registered letter addressed to him at the address at which he ordinarily resides or, in a case in which an address for service has been furnished, at that address.

(2) For the purposes of this section, a company registered under the Companies Acts, 1963 and 1977, shall be deemed to be ordinarily resident at its registered office, and every other body corporate and every unincorporated body shall be deemed to be ordinarily resident at its principal office or place of business.

(3) Where a notice or claim under this Act or any regulations made thereunder is given or served on behalf of a person, it shall be deemed to be given or served by that person.

5.—Every regulation made under this Act shall be laid before each House of the Oireachtas as soon as may be after it is made and, if a resolution annulling the regulation is passed by either such House within the next subsequent 21 days on which that House has sat after the regulation is laid before it, the regulation shall be annulled accordingly, but without prejudice to the validity of anything previously done thereunder.

6. The Rent Restrictions Act, 1960, the Rent Restrictions (Amendment) Act, 1967, and sections 10 and 11 of the Landlord and Tenant (Amendment) Act, 1971, are hereby repealed.

PART II
TENANCIES OF CERTAIN DWELLINGS

7.—(1) In this Part, except where the context otherwise requires—

"the Act of 1980" means the Landlord and Tenant (Amendment) Act, 1980;

"dwelling to which section 8 (1) relates" means a dwelling to which, by virtue of that provision, this Part applies;

"improvement" means any addition to or alteration of a dwelling carried out by the tenant or any of his predecessors in title on or after the 31st day of December, 1960, which adds to the letting value of the dwelling and includes any addition or alteration connected with the provision of any services to the dwelling, but does not include work of repairing (except where such work was the responsibility of the landlord and he failed to carry out the work), painting and decorating or any of them;

"tenant" means the person for the time being entitled to the possession of a dwelling to which section 8 (1) relates and includes a person—

(*a*) who would, at the commencement of this Act, be the tenant of the dwelling if the Rent Restrictions Act, 1960, and the Rent Restrictions (Amendment) Act, 1967, had full force and effect at all times from their passing until such commencement, and

(*b*) who is in possession of the dwelling at such commencement, and

(*c*) whose tenancy is not a tenancy in respect of which an order for possession has been made under section 5 of the Rent Restrictions (Temporary Provisions) Act, 1981.

(2) For the purposes of this Part, a person shall be deemed to be a member of the family of a tenant if—

(*a*) such person is the tenant's father, mother, grandfather, grandmother, step-father, step-mother, father-in-law, mother-in-law, son, daughter, son-in-law, daughter-in-law, nephew, niece, grandson, granddaughter, step-son, step-daughter, brother, sister, half-brother, half-sister, uncle or aunt;

or

(*b*) such person is adopted by the tenant under the Adoption Acts, 1952 to 1976, or is the illegitimate offspring of the tenant (being the mother or the reputed father of such offspring) or is a person who was in *bona fide* residence with the tenant for not less than six years before the tenant's death where the tenant was *in loco parentis* to that person.

8.—(1) Subject to subsection (2), this Part applies to every dwelling which would, at the commencement of this Act, be a controlled dwelling within the meaning of the Rent Restrictions Acts, 1960 to 1981, if those Acts had full force and effect at such commencement, other than such a dwelling held at such commencement under a contract of tenancy for greater than from year to year during such period as it is so held.

(2) Sections 9 and 16 do not apply to—

(*a*) a dwelling let to a person in connection with his continuance in any office, appointment or employment,

or

(*b*) a dwelling let *bona fide* for the temporary convenience or to meet a temporary necessity of the landlord or the tenant.

(3) Where—

(*a*) the entitlement of a tenant to retain possession of a dwelling to which subsection (1) relates ceases to subsist, or

(*b*) the tenant of the dwelling assigns or sublets his tenancy, or

(*c*) the landlord of the dwelling recovers possession of the dwelling,

this Part shall cease to apply to the dwelling.

(4) Paragraphs (*a*) and (*c*) of subsection (3) shall not affect the entitlement of a tenant to compensation under section 15.

9.—(i) Subject to the provisions of this Part, a person (in this section referred to as the original tenant) who, immediately before the commencement of this Act, was a tenant of a dwelling to which section 8 (1) relates (not being a dwelling referred to in section 8 (2)) shall be entitled to retain possession as the tenant of the dwelling and that entitlement shall subsist during the lifetime of that person.

(2) Subject to the provisions of this Part, a person being the spouse of the original tenant shall, upon the death of that tenant, if *bona fide* residing in the dwelling at the time of his death, be entitled to retain possession as the tenant of the dwelling and that entitlement shall subsist during the lifetime of the spouse.

(3) Subject to the provisions of this Part, a person being a member of the family of the original tenant shall—

(*a*) if that tenant dies within the relevant period, upon the death of that tenant,

or

(*b*) where the spouse of that tenant has become the tenant by virtue of subsection (2) and dies within the relevant period, upon the death of the spouse,

if *bona fide* residing in the dwelling at such death, be entitled to retain possession as the tenant of the dwelling and that entitlement shall subsist during the period beginning on the date of such death and ending on the expiration of the relevant period.

(4) Subject to the provisions of this Part, where a member of the family of the original tenant becomes, by virtue of subsection (3) or this subsection, the tenant of the dwelling concerned and dies within the relevant period, a person being another member of that family shall, upon such death, if *bona fide* residing in the dwelling at such death, be entitled to retain possession as the tenant of the dwelling and that entitlement shall subsist during the period beginning on the date of such death and ending on the expiration of the relevant period.

(5) Where, in the circumstances described in subsection (3) or (4), more than one member of the original tenant's family was at the time of the relevant death *bona fide* residing in the dwelling, such one member of the family as may be agreed upon between them or, in default of agreement, as may be selected by the Court shall, subject to the provisions of this Part, be the person entitled to retain possession of the dwelling under this section.

(6) Notwithstanding subsections (3) and (4), where less than five years of the relevant period remain unexpired on the date that a member of the family of the original tenant becomes the tenant of a dwelling under this section, the entitlement of that member to retain possession of the dwelling shall subsist during the period beginning on that date and ending on the expiration of five years.

(7) In this section "relevant period" means the period of twenty years beginning on the commencement of this Act.

(8) Entitlement under this section to retain possession of a dwelling shall cease to subsist where possession of the dwelling is recovered by the landlord.

10.—(1) The tenant of a dwelling to which section 8 (1) relates may surrender the dwelling to the landlord on giving to the landlord not less than one month's notice in writing of his intention to surrender the dwelling.

(2) For the removal of any doubt, it is hereby declared that the surrender of a dwelling under subsection (1) shall, for the purposes of the Family Home Protection Act, 1976, be taken to be a conveyance of an interest in the dwelling.

11.—(1) The terms of every tenancy of a dwelling to which section 8 (1) relates shall be such terms as are agreed between the landlord and the tenant or, in default of agreement, as shall be fixed by the Court.

(2) Whenever, after the commencement of this Act, the rent of a dwelling is increased by agreement between the landlord and the tenant or by the Court, the amount of the increase shall not be payable until—

(*a*) the terms of the tenancy have been set out in written form and signed by the landlord or his agent and a copy thereof has been furnished by the landlord to the tenant, and (*b*) if regulations under section 24 are in force, the landlord has complied with the requirements of such regulations.

12.—(1) Subject to subsection (2), the landlord or the tenant of a dwelling to which section 8 (1) relates may at any time apply to the Court for an order fixing the terms of the tenancy and the Court may make such order as justice may require and such order shall be binding on the landlord and the tenant unless varied by a subsequent order of the Court.

(2) Where the Court has fixed the terms of a tenancy under subsection (1), the landlord or the tenant may not apply to the Court to fix new terms of the tenancy until the expiration of five years from the date of the last order of the Court fixing the terms of the tenancy.

(3) An application under this section may be made notwithstanding any agreement between the landlord and tenant fixing the terms of the tenancy, whether such agreement was entered into before or after the commencement of this Act.

(4) If any dispute, failure or question arises or occurs in the carrying out of an order under this section the Court may, on the application of the landlord or the tenant, make such order as justice may require.

(5) The landlord or tenant making an application under subsection (1) shall give one month's notice in writing to the other party of his intention to make the application.

(6) The landlord shall be liable for the tenant's costs and expenses reasonably and necessarily incurred arising out of an application by the landlord to the Court under this section unless the Court, on consideration of all the circumstances, including the means of the landlord and the tenant, otherwise orders.

13.—(1) Where the terms of a tenancy are fixed by the Court under section 12, the rent of the dwelling shall be the gross rent reduced by an allowance for any improvements, and any such allowance shall be such proportion of the gross rent as is, in the opinion of the Court, attributable to the improvements.

(2) For the purposes of subsection (1), the gross rent shall be the rent which, in the opinion of the Court, would be a just and proper rent having regard to the nature, character and location of the dwelling, the other terms of the tenancy, the means of the landlord and the tenant, the date of purchase of the dwelling by the landlord and the amount paid by him therefor, the length of the tenant's occupancy of the dwelling and the number and ages of the tenant's family residing in the dwelling.

14.—(1) Where the terms of a tenancy are fixed by the Court under section 12, the Court may, in respect of the period from the date of the service of notice of intention under subsection (5) of that section and the date of the order of the Court, order the landlord or the tenant, as the case may require, to pay to the other party an amount not exceeding the difference between the new rent fixed by the Court and the existing rent.

(2) The amount ordered by the Court to be paid under subsection (1) shall be paid in such manner and over such period as the Court may direct having regard to all the circumstances of the case.

15.—(1) The tenant of a dwelling to which section 8 (1) relates shall, upon quitting the dwelling, be entitled to be paid by the landlord compensation for improvements and the amount of the compensation shall be such sum as may be agreed between the landlord and the tenant or, in default of agreement, as shall be determined by the Court.

(2) Where compensation is determined by the Court the amount shall be the capitalised value of such addition to the letting value of the dwelling at the time of quitting which is attributable to the improvements, having regard to the probable life of the improvements and all other relevant circumstances.

(3) Where compensation for improvements is payable the Court may deduct from the compensation as ascertained under subsection (2) such sum as it considers reasonable—

(*a*) if the Court is satisfied that the tenant or his predecessors in title has received from the landlord benefits by way of reduction of rent or otherwise in consideration, expressly or impliedly, of the improvements having been made, or

(*b*) if an order for possession has been granted for a reason specified in section 16 (1) (*a*), (*b*) or (*c*), to compensate the landlord for any rent due or any loss incurred arising from the reasons for which the order for possession was granted.

(4) A tenant seeking compensation under this section shall serve a claim in writing on the landlord either before or after he has quit the dwelling concerned and shall give all particulars relevant to the claim, but a claim may not be served later than three months after such quitting.

(5) Compensation for improvements payable by a landlord under this section shall be payable in such manner and over such period as may be agreed between the landlord and the tenant or as the Court may direct.

(6) A tenant shall not be entitled to compensation under this section—

(*a*) in respect of improvements made in contravention of any obligation of the tenancy agreement under which the dwelling concerned was let unless the Court considers that, in the circumstances, the carrying out of the improvements was reasonable, or

(*b*) where compensation has been paid in respect of the dwelling under Part IV of the Act of 1980.

(7) Where compensation is paid under this section in respect of a dwelling, no right to compensation for improvements to that dwelling shall lie under Part IV of the Act of 1980.

16.—(1) Nothwithstanding the right to retain possession under section 9, the Court may, on the application of the landlord of a dwelling to which section 8 (1) relates (not being a dwelling referred to in section 8 (2), grant an order for the recovery of possesion of the dwelling if the Court considers it reasonable to make the order and—

(*a*) any rent lawfully due by the tenant has not been paid or any other obligation of the tenant under the tenancy has not been fulfilled by him, or

(*b*) any person (being the tenant or any person residing in the dwelling) has been guilty of conduct which the Court is satisfied is a nuisance or annoyance to the landlord or his agent or to adjoining occupiers or has used the dwelling or allowed it to be used for any immoral or illegal purpose (whether or not the person has been convicted of so using it or allowing it to be so used), or

(*c*) the condition of the dwelling has, in the opinion of the Court, deteriorated owing to acts of waste by, or the neglect or default of the tenant or any person residing in the dwelling, or

(*d*) the dwelling is *bona fide* required by the landlord—

(i) for occupation as a residence for himself or any person *bona fide* residing or to reside with him, or

(ii) for occupation as a residence for a person in the wholetime employment of the landlord, or

(iii) in the interests of good estate management, or

(*e*) the landlord requires vacant possession to carry out a scheme of development of property which includes the dwelling and has planning permission for the scheme,

and, as respects recovery of possession under paragraph (*d*) or (*e*), the landlord pays such sum as the Court considers reasonable to meet the expenses incurred by the tenant in quitting the dwelling, together with a sum not exceeding three years' rent of alternative accommodation which is reasonably suited to the residential and other needs of the tenant, his spouse and his family *bona fide* residing with him in the dwelling.

(2) The Court, in considering if it is reasonable to make an order for recovery of possession, shall have regard to the extent (if any) to which the conduct of the landlord contributed to the existence of the grounds upon which he relies in support of his application for recovery of possession.

(3) Nothing in this Part shall prevent a local authority from obtaining possession of a dwelling to which section 8 (1) relates which is reasonably required for the purpose of the execution of their powers, functions and duties.

(4) In this section—

"development" has the meaning assigned by section 3 of the Local Government (Planning and Development) Act, 1963;

"planning permission" means a permission for the development of land where required by and granted under Part IV of the Local Government (Planning and Development) Act, 1963, and, where regulations under section 25 of that Act make provision for outline applications, includes a permission granted on such an application.

17.—(1) Notwithstanding anything in section 15 of the Summary Jurisdiction (Ireland) Act, 1851, every warrant for delivery of possession of, or to enter and give possession of, a dwelling to which section 8 (1) relates (not being a dwelling referred to in section 8 (2)) shall remain in force for six months from the day next after the last day named in the order for delivery of possession or, in the case of a warrant under that Act, from the date of the issue of the warrant, and in either case for such further period or periods, if any, as the Court shall from time to time, whether before or after the expiration of such six months, direct.

(2) Section 15 of the said Act shall apply to such dwelling if the rateable valuation thereof does not exceed ten pounds, notwithstanding that the rent exceeds one pound by the month.

18.—(1) Where an order for the recovery of possession of a dwelling to which section 8 (1) relates is made by the Court or was so made before the commencement of this Act, the Court may, at the time of the order or at any time before the execution thereof, stay execution on the order or postpone the date of possession for such period or periods and subject to such conditions as the Court thinks fit, and if such conditions are complied with the Court may, if it thinks fit, discharge or vary the order.

(2) Where the Court, under subsection (1), stays execution on an order for the recovery of possession or postpones the date of possession, the Court may from time to time, on application which may in case of urgency be made *ex parte*, further stay execution on the order or further postpone the date of possession.

19.—Where it appears to the Court that an order for the recovery of possession of a dwelling to which section 8 (1) relates was obtained by the landlord by misrepresentation or concealment of material facts, the Court may order the landlord to pay to the former tenant such sum as the Court considers reasonable by way of compensation for damage or loss sustained by the tenant as a result of the order for possession.

20.—Where the landlord of a dwelling to which section 8 (1) relates institutes proceedings for the recovery of possession of the dwelling, the acceptance of any sum purporting to be rent by the landlord for the period from the date of the institution of the proceedings to the date on which they are finally determined shall not prejudice his right (if any) to recover possession of the dwelling and, if an order for possession is made, any such sum so accepted shall be treated as mesne profits.

21.—(1) The District Court shall have jurisdiction to hear and determine all issues arising under this Part.

(2) The jurisdiction of the Court shall be exercised by a justice of the District Court for the time being assigned to the district in which is situated the dwelling in relation to which the jurisdiction is exercised.

22.—Where the spouse of the original tenant becomes, under section 9, the tenant of a dwelling, the interest of the spouse shall not, for the purposes of any enactments relating to settled land, be regarded as having been acquired under a settlement.

23.—(1) The Minister for Social Welfare may, with the consent of the Minister for Finance, make regulations for the payment out of moneys provided by the Oireachtas of allowances to the tenants of dwellings to which section 8 (1) relates who would otherwise suffer hardship by reason of increases in the rents of their dwellings.

(2) Entitlement to an allowance and the amount and the payment thereof shall be subject to such conditions and limitations as may be specified in the regulations.

(3) Subsections (2) and (3) of section 3 of the Social Welfare (Consolidation) Act, 1981, shall have effect in relation to regulations under this section and the regulations may apply (with or without modification), or make provisions corresponding (with or without modification) to, any other provisions of, or any provisions made under, that Act.

(4) Any expenses incurred by the Minister for Social Welfare or any other Minister in carrying this section into effect shall, to such extent as may be sanctioned by the Minister for Finance, be paid out of moneys provided by the Oireachtas.

PART III

RENTED DWELLINGS-REGISTRATION, RENT BOOKS, STANDARDS.

24.—(1) The Minister shall make regulations requiring the landlords of any class of dwelling let for rent to register the tenancy of each dwelling with the housing authority in whose functional area the dwelling is situated and to furnish such particulars as the regulations may specify, including the name and address of the landlord and of the tenant and the amount of the rent.

(2) The regulations shall contain such provisions as the Minister considers necessary for the purposes of this section.

(3) The regulations shall provide that an application to register a dwelling shall be accompanied by such fee as may be prescribed from time to time by the Minister by regulations.

(4) A housing authority shall keep a register (in this section referred to as the register) for the purposes of this section in respect of all dwellings in the functional

area of the authority to which regulations under this section relate and shall make all such entries therein as may from time to time be appropriate in accordance with this section and regulations made by the Minister.

(5) The register shall be kept at the offices of the housing authority and shall be available for inspection during normal office hours.

(6) A document purporting to be a copy of an entry in the register and to be certified by an officer of the housing authority as a correct copy shall be *prima facie* evidence of the entry and it shall not be necessary to prove the signature of such officer or that he was in fact such officer.

(7) Evidence of an entry in the register may be given by the production of a copy thereof certified in accordance with subsection (6) and it shall not be necessary to produce the register.

(8) Where an application is made to a housing authority for a copy of an entry in the register, the copy shall be issued to the applicant on payment by him of such fee (if any) in respect of each entry as the Minister may, from time to time, prescribe by regulations.

(9) All fees received by a housing authority by virtue of regulations under this section shall be paid, in the case of a council of a county, into the county fund and, in the case of a corporation of a county or other borough or the council of an urban district, into the municipal fund.

25.—(1) The Minister shall make regulations requiring the landlords of any class of dwelling let for rent to provide the tenant of a dwelling of such class with a rent book or other similar document for use in respect of the dwelling.

(2) The regulations shall prescribe, in relation to the rent book or similar document—

(*a*) the particulars to be contained therein,

(*b*) requirements regarding its proper use, and

(*c*) such other matters as the Minister considers necessary.

26.—(1) The Minister shall make regulations prescribing standards for any class of dwelling let for rent.

(2) In particular, the regulations shall prescribe standards in relation to—

(*a*) the quality and condition of the accommodation, furnishings and appliances,

(*b*) the maintenance of the dwellings in good repair and in an adequate state of cleanliness,

(*c*) ventilation and lighting,

(*d*) the provision of water supplies, sanitary facilities and drainage, (*e*) heating and cooking, and

(*f*) accommodation for the storage of and facilities for the preparation of food.

(3) A person authorised for the purpose by the housing authority may at all reasonable times enter and inspect any dwelling to which regulations under this section apply.

(4) Where a requirement of a regulation is not being complied with, the housing authority may, after giving not less than 21 days notice in writing to the landlord and the tenant of the dwelling concerned, carry out any work necessary to ensure that the dwelling complies with the requirements of the regulations and may recover as a simple contract debt in a court of competent jurisdiction from the landlord any expenses reasonably incurred by the authority in that behalf.

(5) A landlord upon whom a notice is served under subsection (4) may appeal to the District Court in the District Court district in which the dwelling concerned is situate to have the notice set aside and no work shall be carried out by the housing authority until the appeal is determined.

(6) Upon the coming into operation of regulations under this section relating to a class of dwelling, any bye-laws under section 70 of the Housing Act, 1966, in force in relation to that class of dwelling shall cease to have effect and no bye-laws shall thereafter be made under that section in relation to that class of dwelling.

27.—(1) A person who obstructs a person duly authorised under section 26 (3) and a person who contravenes a regulation under this Part shall be guilty of an offence and shall be liable on summary conviction to a fine not exceeding £500.

(2) Where an offence under subsection (1) which is committed by a body corporate is proved to have been committed with the consent or connivance of, or to be attributable to any neglect on the part of, any person (or any person acting on his behalf) being a director, manager or secretary of such body, that person or the person so acting, as the case may be, shall be guilty of that offence.

(3) The housing authority shall be responsible for the enforcement of regulations under this Part.

(4) An offence under this section may be prosecuted by the housing authority.

(5) Notwithstanding section 10 (4) of the Petty Sessions (Ireland) Act, 1851, proceedings for an offence under this section may be instituted at any time within twelve months after the date of the offence.

Housing (Private Rented Dwellings) (Amendment) Act, 1983

Number 22 of 1983

AN ACT TO MAKE NEW PROVISION FOR THE FIXING OF THE TERMS OF THE TENANCIES OF CERTAIN DWELLINGS AND FOR THAT PURPOSE TO PROVIDE FOR THE ESTABLISHMENT OF A RENT TRIBUNAL, FOR THE APPOINTMENT BY HOUSING AUTHORITIES OF RENT OFFICERS AND FOR THE FUNCTIONS OF THE TRIBUNAL AND RENT OFFICERS, TO MAKE CERTAIN CONSEQUENTIAL AMENDMENTS TO THE HOUSING (PRIVATE RENTED DWELLINGS) ACT, 1982, AND TO PROVIDE FOR OTHER RELATED MATTERS. [13*th July*, 1983]

BE IT ENACTED BY THE OIREACHTAS AS FOLLOWS:

1.—(1) In this Act, except where the context otherwise requires—

"the Act of 1982" means the Housing (Private Rented Dwellings) Act, 1982;

"rent officer" means a rent officer appointed under section 6(2);

"the Tribunal" has the meaning assigned to it by section 2(1).

(2) The Act of 1982 and this Act shall be construed together as one.

(3) A reference in this Act to a section is to a section of this Act unless it is indicated that reference to some other provision is intended.

(4) A reference in this Act to a subsection or paragraph is to a subsection or paragraph of the provision in which the reference occurs unless it is indicated that reference to some other provision is intended.

2.—(1) There shall be established on such day as the Minister may by order appoint a body to be known as the Rent Tribunal (in this Act referred to as the Tribunal) to perform the functions assigned to it by this Act.

(2) The Tribunal shall consist of the following members, namely, a chairman and so many vice-chairmen and ordinary members as the Minister, with the consent of the Minister for the Public Service, considers necessary from time to time for the performance by the Tribunal of its functions under this Act.

(3) (*a*) The chairman, vice-chairmen and the ordinary members shall be

appointed by the Minister by order.

(*b*) The Minister may by order revoke or amend an order under paragraph (a) or this paragraph.

(*c*) An order under this subsection shall be published in *Iris Oifigiúil* as soon as may be after it is made.

(4) The Minister, with the consent of the Minister for the Public Service, may from time to time appoint from among his officers so many persons as he considers necessary to assist the Tribunal in the performance of its functions under this Act.

3.—(1) A person who, for the time being, is entitled under the Standing Orders of either House of the Oireachtas to sit therein or is a representative in the Assembly of the European Communities or a member of a local authority shall be disqualified from being appointed to be a member of the Tribunal.

(2) A member of the Tribunal, who—

(*a*) is nominated either as a member of Seanad Éireann or for election to either House of the Oireachtas, or

(*b*) is either nominated for election to the Assembly of the European Communities or appointed to be a representative in that Assembly, or

(*c*) becomes a member of a local authority,

shall thereupon cease to be a member of the Tribunal.

(3) In this section "local authority" means the council of a county, the corporation of a county or other borough, the council of an urban district or the commissioners of a town.

4.—(1) The Tribunal shall provide itself with a seal.

(2) The seal of the Tribunal shall be authenticated by the signature of the chairman of the Tribunal or of a vice-chairman or ordinary member thereof authorised by the Tribunal to act in that behalf or a person appointed under section 2 (4) authorised by the Tribunal to act in that behalf.

(3) Judicial notice shall be taken of the seal of the Tribunal, and every document purporting to be an instrument made by the Tribunal and to be sealed with the seal (purporting to be authenticated in accordance with this section) of the Tribunal shall be received in evidence and shall be deemed to be such instrument without further proof unless the contrary is shown.

5.—(1) The landlord or the tenant of a dwelling to which section 8 (1) of the Act of 1982 relates may, subject to subsection (2), at any time—

(*a*) apply to the Tribunal to fix the terms of the tenancy, or

(*b*) where an order has been made under section 6 (1), apply to the housing authority in whose functional area the dwelling is situated to have the terms of the tenancy fixed by a rent officer,

and the terms of the tenancy shall be determined by the Tribunal or the rent officer, as the case may be, and shall, subject to this Act, be binding on the landlord and the tenant unless new terms are fixed under this Act.

(2) An application under subsection (1) may be made notwithstanding any agreement between the landlord and the tenant fixing the terms of the tenancy, whether such agreement was entered into before or after the commencement of this section.

(3) (*a*) Where the terms of a tenancy of a dwelling have been or are, before or after the commencement of this section, fixed by the Court under the Act of 1982 or are fixed under this Act, an application under subsection (1) may not be made until the expiration of four years and nine months from the date on which the terms were so fixed except where the landlord has carried out improvements to the dwelling.

(*b*) In this subsection "improvements" means any addition to or alteration of a dwelling which adds to the letting value of the dwelling and includes any addition or alteration connected with the provision of any services to the dwelling, but does not include work of repairing, decorating or normal maintenance.

(4) If any dispute or question arises in the interpretation of a determination by the Tribunal or a rent officer under this Act, the Tribunal or the rent officer, as the case may be, shall, on the application of the landlord or the tenant, resolve the matter.

(5) The landlord or tenant making an application under subsection (1) shall give one month's notice in writing to the other party of his intention to make the application.

(6) No application may be made under section 12(1) of the Act of 1982 after the commencement of this section.

6.—(1) The Minister may by order direct that all applications for the purpose of fixing the terms of tenancies of dwellings to which section 8(1) of the Act of 1982 relates shall be made to housing authorities for determination by rent officers appointed for that purpose by housing authorities.

(2) A housing authority, on the making of an order under subsection (1) shall, and may from time to time thereafter, appoint from among the officers of the housing authority or of another housing authority so many persons as they consider necessary to be rent officers for the purposes of this Act.

(3) A housing authority may at any time terminate an appointment made under subsection (2).

(4) Housing authorities may make arrangements for the joint discharge of their functions under this Act.

(5) Where it appears to the Minister that an agreement under section 59 of the Local Government Act, 1955, ought to be made between housing authorities for the purposes of their functions under this Act, he may, after affording an opportunity to the authorities concerned to make representations to him, require them to enter into such agreement.

(6) The Minister may direct that any such agreement shall contain such terms as he may specify and the authority concerned shall comply with any directions given by the Minister.

(7) A rent officer appointed pursuant to such an agreement shall be the rent officer for the functional areas of the authorities concerned.

(8) An order under subsection (1) may contain provisions relating to applications made under section 5(1) to the Tribunal, including provisions for the withdrawing of such applications, for the manner in which they are to be withdrawn and for the making of new applications to housing authorities.

7.—(1) The terms of every tenancy of a dwelling to which section 8(1) of the Act of 1982 relates shall be such terms as are agreed between the landlord and the tenant or, in default of agreement—

(*a*) as have been or are, before or after the commencement of this section, fixed by the Court under section 12 of the Act of 1982, or

(*b*) as shall be fixed by the Tribunal or a rent officer under this Act.

(2) Whenever, after the commencement of this section, the rent of a dwelling is increased by agreement between the landlord and the tenant or by the Tribunal or a rent officer under this Act, the amount of the increase shall not be payable until—

(*a*) the terms of the tenancy have been set out in written form and signed by the landlord or his agent and a copy thereof has been furnished by the landlord to the tenant, and

(*b*) the landlord has complied with the requirements of any regulations under section 24 of the Act of 1982 for the time being in force.

8.—(1) Where the rent of a dwelling is fixed by the Tribunal or a rent officer, the new rent shall, subject to subsection (2) and section 7, apply from the first gale day after the date on which the landlord has complied with the requirements of any regulations under section 24 of the Act of 1982 for the time being in force.

(2) Where, on an application under this Act by a landlord or tenant, the rent of a dwelling is fixed and the existing rent was fixed under the Act of 1982 or this Act, the new rent shall apply—

(*a*) in the case of an application (other than an application made by virtue of section 5(3)) from whichever of the following dates is the later—

(i) the first gale day after the date referred to in subsection (1), or

(ii) the date which is five years after the date from which the existing rent first applied, and

(*b*) in the case of an application made by virtue of section 5(3), the first gale day after the date referred to in subsection (1).

9.—(1) Section 12 (1) of the Act of 1982 is hereby amended by the insertion after "order of the Court" of "or unless new terms of the tenancy are fixed under the Housing (Private Rented Dwellings) (Amendment) Act, 1983".

(2) Section 13 of the Act of 1982 shall have effect where the terms of a tenancy are fixed by the Tribunal or a rent officer under this Act in the same manner as it has effect where such terms are fixed by the Court under section 12 of that Act and, accordingly, the references in the said section 13 to the opinion of the Court shall be construed as including, as the case may require, references to the opinion of the Tribunal or the opinion of the rent officer.

(3) The reference in section 13(2) of the Act of 1982 to the means of the tenant shall be taken to refer, and always to have referred, to the actual means of the tenant.

10.—(1) Where a landlord or tenant has made an application to the Court under section 12(1) of the Act of 1982 and, at the commencement of section 5 of this Act, the matter has not come on for hearing before the Court, the applicant may, if the other party consents, withdraw the application and may make a new application under this Act to the Tribunal or a housing authority, as the case may be.

(2) Where an application is withdrawn under subsection (1), the notice given by the applicant under section 12(5) of the Act of 1982 to the other party of his intention to make the application shall, for the purposes of a new application under this Act, be deemed to be a notice duly given to the other party under section 5(5) of this Act.

11.—(1) A landlord or tenant may, in accordance with regulations under section 15, appeal to the Tribunal against the determination of a rent officer fixing the terms of a tenancy under section 5 and the Tribunal shall fix the terms of the tenancy.

(2) Where the terms of a tenancy are varied by the Tribunal under subsection (1), the terms as so varied shall be binding on the landlord and the tenant.

(3) Where the rent fixed by a rent officer exceeds the rent fixed by the Tribunal on an appeal under subsection (1), the amount of any excess paid by the tenant—

(*a*) may be deducted from any rent payable by him to the landlord, or

(*b*) shall be recoverable by him as a simple contract debt in a court of competent jurisdiction.

(4) The making of an appeal under subsection (l) shall not prevent the registration of a dwelling in accordance with the determination of the rent officer for the purpose of compliance with section 7(2)(b).

12.—(1) Where the terms of a tenancy are fixed by the Tribunal under this Act, the Tribunal may, on an application to it by either the landlord or the tenant and if it considers it reasonable to do so, order the landlord or the tenant, as the case may be, to pay to the other party an amount not exceeding the difference between the existing rent and the new rent fixed by the Tribunal in respect of—

(*a*) where an application is withdrawn under section 10(1) and a new application is made under this Act, the period from the date of the notice referred to in section 10(2) to the date of the fixing of the terms by the Tribunal, or

(*b*) where an appeal is made under section 11(1) against the determination of a rent officer, the period from the date of the determination by the rent officer to the date of the fixing of the terms by the Tribunal.

(2) Any amount ordered by the Tribunal to be paid under subsection (1) shall be paid in such manner and over such period as the Tribunal may direct having regard to all the circumstances of the case.

(3) A decision of the Tribunal under subsection (1) shall be final and conclusive and no appeal shall lie against the decision except to the High Court on a question of law.

13.—(1) A landlord or tenant may appeal to the High Court on a question of law within three months, or such longer period as that Court may allow, after the determination by the Tribunal of the terms of a tenancy under section 5 or on an appeal under section 11.

(2) The Minister may, at the request of the Tribunal, refer to the High Court a question of law arising on an application or appeal to it under this Act and the Minister may be represented at the hearing.

14.—(1) Where a member of the Tribunal has a beneficial interest in a dwelling in respect of which an application under section 5(1) or an appeal under section 11 is made, or has any other interest in the application or appeal which would be likely to influence him in relation to the determination of the terms of the tenancy or the decision on the appeal, as the case may be, the member shall—

(*a*) disclose to the Tribunal the nature of his interest,

(*b*) take no part in the discussion on, or consideration of, the application or appeal,

(*c*) neither vote nor otherwise act as a member of the Tribunal in relation to the determination of the terms of the tenancy or the decision on the appeal, as the case may be.

(2) Where a rent officer has a beneficial interest in a dwelling in respect of which an application under section 5(1) is made, or has any other interest in the application which would be likely to influence him in determining the terms of the tenancy,

he—

(*a*) shall neither make nor seek to influence the determination of the tenancy, and

(*b*) shall inform the manager of the housing authority of his interest.

(3) The manager of the housing authority, upon being so informed, shall refer the application to another rent officer of the authority or, if there is no such other officer, to another housing authority for determination by a rent officer of that authority.

(4) Where an officer of the Tribunal has a beneficial interest in a dwelling to which an application or appeal mentioned in subsection (3) relates, or has any other interest in the application or appeal which is material to the outcome thereof, he shall—

(*a*) neither influence nor seek to influence the determination of the terms of the tenancy of the dwelling or the decision on the appeal, as the case may be, and

(*b*) disclose to the Tribunal the nature of his interest and comply with any directions the Tribunal may give in relation to the matter.

(5) For the purposes of this section, a person shall be regarded as having a beneficial interest in a dwelling if—

(*a*) he or his spouse is the landlord or the tenant of the dwelling, or

(*b*) he or his spouse, or a nominee of either of them, is a member of a company or other body which is the landlord of the dwelling, or

(*c*) he or his spouse is in partnership with, or in the employment of, a person who is either the landlord or the tenant of the dwelling.

(6) For the purposes of this section, a person shall not be regarded as having a beneficial interest in a dwelling, or an interest in an application or appeal which would be likely to influence him, by reason only of an interest of his, or of a company or any other body mentioned in subsection (5), which is so remote or insignificant that it cannot reasonably be regarded as likely to influence him.

(7) (*a*) A person who has a beneficial interest in a dwelling and contravenes or fails to comply with a requirement of this section shall be guilty of an offence and shall be liable on summary conviction to a fine not exceeding £500.

(*b*) In any proceedings for an offence under this subsection, it shall be a good defence for the person charged to prove that at the time of the alleged offence he did not know and had no reason to believe that—

(i) he had a beneficial interest in the dwelling, or

(ii) the beneficial interest to which the alleged offence relates was one in relation to which a requirement of this section applied.

(c) Proceedings for an offence under this subsection shall not be initiated save by or with the consent of the Director of Public Prosecutions.

(8) A member of the Tribunal who is convicted of an offence under subsection (7) shall, on such conviction, cease to be a member.

(9) Where a person who has a beneficial interest in a dwelling to which an application or appeal to which this section relates contravenes or fails to comply with a requirement of this section, such contravention or failure shall render invalid the determination of the application or the decision on the appeal, as the case may be.

(10) (*a*) Where a determination under section 5(1) by the Tribunal or a rent officer is rendered invalid by virtue of subsection (9), the application to which the determination relates shall again be determined by the Tribunal or a rent officer, as the case may be.

(*b*) Where a decision by the Tribunal on an appeal under section 11 is rendered invalid by virtue of subsection (9), the appeal shall be again decided by the Tribunal.

(*c*) For the purposes of this Act—

(i) the date of a new determination under paragraph (*a*) by the Tribunal or a rent officer shall be taken to be the date of the invalid determination, and

(ii) the date of a new decision under paragraph (*b*) by the Tribunal shall be taken to be the date of the invalid decision.

(11) If, by reason of a new determination or decision under subsection (10), any amount is owed to a landlord or tenant, such amount may be recovered as a simple contract debt in a court of competent jurisdiction.

15.—(1) The Minister may by regulations provide for—

(*a*) subject to subsection (3), the terms and conditions of appointment (including remuneration, if any, and allowances) and the tenure of office of the members of the Tribunal,

(*b*) the manner in which the Tribunal, housing authorities and rent officers shall perform their functions under this Act, and

(*c*) the enabling of the Tribunal, housing authorities and rent officers to perform such functions effectively.

(2) Regulations under this section may include provisions relating to all or any of the following matters:

(*a*) the procedure for making applications under section 5(1)(*a*) and appeals under section 11 to the Tribunal, the determination of such applications and appeals (including provisions that they may be determined without recourse to an oral hearing) and the notification of the determinations;

(*b*) the procedure for making applications to a housing authority under section 5(1)(*b*), the determination of such applications (including provisions that they may be determined without recourse to an oral hearing) and the notification of the determinations;

(*c*) the meetings of the Tribunal and the procedure at such meetings, including provisions that the Tribunal may act by divisions and the conditions under which it may do so;

(*d*) the charging and payment of fees in respect of applications to the Tribunal and housing authorities;

(*e*) the furnishing to the Tribunal or a rent officer by an applicant or appellant, as the case may be, of any specified information relating to the application or appeal and the production by the applicant or appellant of evidence to verify any particulars or information given by him;

(*f*) the engaging of consultants and advisers by a housing authority to assist a rent officer or by the Tribunal;

(*g*) the making available to the landlord and the tenant concerned of any written submissions to the Tribunal or a rent officer, as the case may be;

(*h*) the furnishing by a rent officer to the Tribunal of documents or other matter in relation to an appeal from a determination by him;

(*i*) the circumstances and conditions under which the Tribunal or a rent officer may declare that an application or appeal, as the case may be, shall be regarded as having been abandoned;

(*j*) where an application or appeal is, in the opinion of the Tribunal or a rent officer, as the case may be, being unnecessarily delayed, the circumstances and conditions under which the application or appeal may be determined or be regarded as having been abandoned;

(*k*) the award by the Tribunal of costs and expenses and the payment thereof;

(*l*) the making by the Tribunal of an annual report to the Minister;

(*m*) the furnishing from time to time by the Tribunal or a housing authority to the Minister of information relating to the performance of their functions under this Act and the furnishing, at any time at the Minister's request, of such information;

(*n*) the regulating of the finances of, and the keeping and auditing of the accounts of, the Tribunal;

(*o*) matters ancillary or incidental to any of the foregoing matters.

(3) Regulations relating to the matters specified in subsection (1)(*a*) shall be

made only with the consent of the Minister for the Public Service.

(4) The Public Offices Fees Act, 1879, shall not apply in respect of fees payable by virtue of this Act.

16.—(1) Any person who, in connection with an application to the Tribunal or a housing authority under section 5(1) or an appeal to the Tribunal under section 11, in the course of the determination by the Tribunal or a rent officer of the terms of a tenancy or in the course of the hearing of such appeal, gives any information, either orally or in writing, which he knows to be false or misleading, shall be guilty of an offence and shall be liable on summary conviction to a fine not exceeding £500.

(2) Where an offence under this section which is committed by a body corporate is proved to have been committed with the consent or connivance of, or to be attributable to any neglect on the part of, any person (or any person acting on his behalf) being a director, manager or secretary of such body, that person or the person so acting, as the case may be, shall be guilty of that offence.

17.—(1) A member of the Tribunal, a rent officer or a person authorised for the purpose by the Tribunal or a housing authority may, for the purpose of determining an application or appeal under this Act, at all reasonable times, enter and inspect a dwelling in respect of which an application under section 5(1) or an appeal under section 11 has been made.

(2) A person who obstructs a member of the Tribunal, a rent officer or a person authorised under subsection (1) entering or carrying out an inspection under that subsection shall be guilty of an offence under section 27 of the Act of 1982.

18.—Section 4 of the Act of 1982 shall apply to notices and claims under this Act or under regulations made under this Act.

19.—Every regulation made by the Minister under this Act shall be laid before each House of the Oireachtas as soon as may be after it is made and, if a resolution annulling the regulation is passed by either such House within the next subsequent 21 days on which that House has sat after the regulation is laid before it, the regulation shall be annulled accordingly, but without prejudice to the validity of anything previously done thereunder.

20.—The Minister may, with the consent of the Minister for Finance, in each financial year make, out of moneys provided by the Oireachtas, grants to a housing authority to meet the expenses reasonably and necessarily incurred by the authority in the exercise by the authority and by rent officers of the authority of their functions under this Act.

21.—The expenses incurred by the Minister in the administration of this Act shall be paid out of moneys provided by the Oireachtas.

22.—(1) This Act may be cited as the Housing (Private Rented Dwellings) (Amendment) Act, 1983.

(2) The Housing (Private Rented Dwellings) Act, 1982, and this Act may be cited together as the Housing (Private Rented Dwellings) Acts, 1982 and 1983.

(3) This Act shall come into operation on such day or days as the Minister, by order or orders, may fix either generally or with reference to any particular purpose or provision and different days may be so fixed for different purposes and different provisions.

Table of cases

Table of statutes

Housing (Private Rented Dwellings) Act 1982 (contd.)

Housing (Private Rented Dwellings) (Amendment) Act 1983

Table of statutory instruments

Index